SHADOW WORK

FOR

Angry BLACK WOMEN

Reclaim Your Power, Heal Your Pain, and Celebrate Your True Self with Ancestral Practices, Meditation and Sacred Self-Care (bonus 369 Manifestation Method)

BW Journey

UNLOCK YOUR MANIFESTATION POTENTIAL!

Scan the QR code below to claim your **FREE** copy of

"PROJECT 369: WORKBOOK

Activate The Law of Attraction and Manifest the Life of Your Dreams."

✦ Why You Need This Workbook:

- Learn how to align with the energy of your desires.
- Activate the Law of Attraction using proven 369 techniques.
- Transform your thoughts into reality and manifest the life you've always dreamed of!

Start manifesting your dreams today!

CONTENTS FOR *BW*

Introduction

Welcome to ***Shadow Work for Angry Black Women: Reclaim Your Power, Heal Your Pain, and Celebrate Your True Self.***

This book is not just a guide; it's an invitation to embark on a transformative journey of healing, growth, and self-discovery. Whether you picked up this book because you're seeking to release buried pain, reconnect with your authentic self, or simply find a space where your voice is acknowledged and celebrated, know that you're in the right place.

THIS IS YOUR STORY, YOUR JOURNEY, AND YOUR PROCESS. As you move through the chapters, you'll encounter reflections, practices, and exercises designed to help you uncover hidden parts of yourself, confront the sources of your anger and pain, and ultimately transform them into power and purpose.

What This Book Offers

- *A Safe Space to Explore*

Anger is often misunderstood, especially for Black women, who are frequently judged or silenced when expressing it. Here, anger isn't something to suppress or fear—it's a signal, a teacher, and a catalyst for change. This book will help you explore the roots of your anger, understand its deeper messages, and channel it into healing and empowerment.

- *Interactive Exercises*

Throughout the book, you'll find spaces intentionally left blank—these are yours to fill. These sections are designed for you to engage directly with the material, answer reflective questions, and journal your thoughts. Writing down your responses creates a tangible record of your growth and helps you process emotions more deeply. Think of these spaces as a personal conversation between you and the most authentic version of yourself.

- *A Holistic Approach*

Healing isn't one-size-fits-all, and this book acknowledges that. You'll explore a variety of tools, from journaling and meditation to ancestral rituals and affirmations, so you can choose the practices that resonate most with you.

- *A Celebration of Identity*

This book honors the unique experiences of Black women, weaving in cultural and ancestral wisdom to ground your healing in the richness of your heritage. It's a reminder that you don't walk this journey alone—your ancestors' strength flows through you, and their resilience is part of your legacy.

How to Use This Book

- *Take Your Time*

Healing is not a race. There's no "right" way to move through these pages. Some chapters may resonate deeply, while others may challenge you. Honor where you are and give yourself permission to move at your own pace.

- *Engage Fully*

Use the spaces provided to answer questions, reflect on your feelings, or even sketch your thoughts. There's no judgment here—this is your personal journey, and your answers are for your eyes only.

- *Be Honest with Yourself*

Growth begins with truth. Be courageous in exploring your emotions and experiences, even when it feels uncomfortable.

- *Revisit as Needed*

Healing isn't linear, and neither is this book. You may find yourself revisiting chapters or exercises as you uncover new layers of understanding. That's not just okay—it's part of the process.

What You'll Gain

By the end of this book, you will:

- Understand the roots of your anger and how it connects to your personal and generational experiences.
- Learn tools to process and release pain, setting boundaries and reclaiming your emotional freedom.
- Connect with your ancestors' wisdom and strength to guide your healing.
- Celebrate your identity, embracing all aspects of yourself with compassion and love.

A Final Note

Healing is a courageous act, and by opening this book, you've already taken a powerful step. Remember that this is a journey, not a destination. Some days will feel heavy, while others will bring lightness and clarity. Whatever you feel along the way is valid, and every step forward—no matter how small—is worth celebrating.

As you begin, take a deep breath and remind yourself: I am worthy of healing, growth, and joy. This book is your companion on that journey, and every page is here to support you in becoming the fullest, most empowered version of yourself.

Let's begin.

Part 1: Reclaim Your Power

Chapter 1: The Weight of Anger

How Society Misunderstands Black Women

Anger is an emotion often misunderstood, especially when it comes to Black women. Society has long imposed stereotypes that frame Black women's anger as irrational, aggressive, or unwarranted. Terms like "angry Black woman" are frequently used to silence or dismiss valid emotions, overshadowing the real experiences and systemic injustices that often fuel this anger. This chapter is an invitation to redefine anger—not as something to suppress or feel ashamed of, but as a valid and powerful emotion that can lead to personal empowerment and social change.

Understanding the Roots of the Misunderstanding

For centuries, societal structures have worked to control and manipulate the image of Black women, often painting them as overly emotional or hostile when they express frustration or hurt. This perception is rooted in:

- **Historical stereotypes:** From the "Sapphire" caricature of the 19th century to modern portrayals in media, Black women have been labeled as loud, combative, or difficult. These narratives are not only unfair but dehumanizing.
- **Systemic injustice:** Black women face unique layers of oppression at the intersection of race and gender. When they voice their discontent about these issues, society

often shifts the focus to their tone or delivery rather than the root cause of their pain.

As a result, many Black women learn to internalize anger, fearing that expressing it might lead to professional consequences, strained relationships, or even personal safety risks. But this suppression comes at a cost—it can manifest as anxiety, depression, or physical health issues, all while disconnecting women from their true selves.

Reclaiming Anger as a Source of Power

Anger is not inherently negative. In fact, it is a natural response to feeling violated, unheard, or marginalized. When channelled effectively, anger can be a force for transformation, both personally and collectively. Here's how to start shifting your perspective:

- **Validate Your Feelings:** Acknowledge that your anger is valid. It is a sign that something in your environment is not aligned with your values or needs.
- **Ask yourself:** *What is my anger trying to tell me? What boundary has been crossed?*
- **Embrace Anger as a Catalyst:** History is filled with examples of Black women who have transformed their anger into activism, art, and meaningful change. Figures like Audre Lorde and bell hooks remind us that anger, when understood and harnessed, can be a tool for empowerment and justice.
- **Separate Anger from Aggression:** Recognize that anger does not have to result in harm or aggression. It can instead motivate clear communication, inspire action, or push you toward deeper self-reflection.

Practical Exercises for Honoring Your Anger

Here are some steps to help you begin reframing your anger:

Journaling Your Triggers:

- ✓ Write about the moments that made you angry this week. WRITE IT HERE:

....

....

....

....

....

....

- ✓ Reflect on the underlying causes: *Was it a broken promise, an act of disrespect, or a systemic issue?*

....

....

Anger Visualization:

- ✓ Sit quietly and picture your anger as a flame.
- ✓ Imagine yourself controlling the flame, using it to light a path forward instead of letting it consume you.

Channeling Through Creativity:

- ✓ Paint, draw, or write poetry that expresses your frustration and turns it into something constructive.

Final Thoughts

Black women's anger has often been weaponized against them, but it is time to reclaim it as a powerful, necessary emotion. By embracing and understanding your anger, you can begin to unearth the deeper truths behind it and use it to fuel your growth, healing, and resistance.

In the next chapter, we will explore how breaking free from the "Strong Black Woman" archetype can open the door to vulnerability, authenticity, and self-compassion.

Chapter 2: Breaking Free from the Strong Black Woman Archetype

The archetype of the "Strong Black Woman" is a double-edged sword. While it may symbolize resilience, perseverance, and the ability to overcome adversity, it often comes at a significant cost. Black women are frequently expected to bear burdens in silence, suppress emotions, and prioritize the needs of others above their own. This chapter explores the origins of this myth, its impact on mental and emotional health, and how embracing vulnerability can lead to deeper strength and authenticity.

The Origins of the Strong Black Woman Myth

The "Strong Black Woman" archetype has deep historical roots, stemming from:

➢ **Survival during slavery and systemic oppression:** Black women were forced into roles of caretaker, laborer, and emotional support under unimaginable conditions, leaving little room for emotional expression.

➢ **Cultural narratives of self-sacrifice:** Over time, strength became a badge of honor, passed down through generations as a survival mechanism.

➢ **Media representations:** Modern portrayals in film, television, and literature often celebrate Black women as unbreakable, shouldering the weight of the world without complaint.

While these narratives may seem empowering on the surface, they often fail to acknowledge the toll they take on emotional well-being.

The Cost of Always Being Strong

The "Strong Black Woman" archetype may appear empowering on the surface, but the pressure to embody this ideal can take a significant toll on mental, emotional, and physical well-being. When society expects you to be endlessly resilient, self-sufficient, and unshakable, the very humanity that makes you complex and whole is often overlooked. Over time, this expectation can lead to profound challenges that affect every aspect of your life.

Emotional Suppression

One of the most immediate and insidious effects of constantly performing strength is the suppression of your emotions. The unspoken rule of this archetype is that vulnerability is a weakness—something to be hidden rather than embraced. As a result:

Unprocessed emotions accumulate: Feelings of sadness, fear, anger, or frustration are buried rather than addressed, creating a growing reservoir of unresolved pain.

Isolation becomes the norm: When you believe you must always present as strong, it becomes harder to share your struggles with others, leaving you feeling emotionally disconnected and alone.

<u>Emotional numbness develops:</u> Over time, the act of masking your true feelings can make it difficult to even recognize or name your emotions, leading to a sense of detachment from yourself.

Suppressing your emotions doesn't make them disappear; it simply postpones the moment they demand to be acknowledged—often in ways that feel overwhelming or destabilizing.

Burnout and Exhaustion

Carrying the weight of everyone else's needs while ignoring your own is a direct path to burnout. The expectation that you must be the rock in every situation leaves little room for rest, support, or self-care. This can manifest as:

<u>Physical fatigue:</u> The body reflects emotional and mental strain, often through persistent tiredness, headaches, or other stress-related ailments.

<u>Mental exhaustion:</u> Constantly solving problems, managing crises, and putting others first can drain your mental energy, leaving you feeling scatterbrained or unable to focus.

<u>A loss of joy:</u> Burnout often erodes your ability to enjoy activities or moments that once brought you happiness, replacing them with a sense of obligation or numbness.

The relentless pursuit of strength without rest or reprieve ultimately leaves you depleted, making it harder to show up for yourself or anyone else.

Barriers to Intimacy

When strength becomes synonymous with silence and self-reliance, it creates significant challenges in building and maintaining intimate relationships. True intimacy requires openness, trust, and vulnerability—qualities that the "Strong Black Woman" archetype discourages. This can result in:

Emotional walls: To protect yourself from judgment or perceived weakness, you may withhold your true feelings, making it harder for others to connect with the real you.

Unbalanced relationships: If you're always the giver—offering support, advice, or care—it can create dynamics where your needs are overlooked or dismissed.

Loneliness within relationships: Even surrounded by friends or family, you may feel unseen or misunderstood because you've been taught to hide your struggles.

These barriers don't just affect romantic relationships; they can also strain friendships, family bonds, and professional connections.

The Urgency of Redefining Strength

Living under the constant pressure to be strong is not sustainable, nor is it fair. It asks you to deny the fullness of your humanity—the moments of fear, sadness, or vulnerability that make you whole.

Redefining strength involves embracing a more balanced and compassionate approach to life. This means:

Allowing yourself to feel: Strength isn't the absence of emotion—it's the courage to acknowledge and honor your feelings.

Asking for help: True strength is knowing when to lean on others and recognizing that support is a sign of wisdom, not weakness.

Setting boundaries: Saying no to what drains you and yes to what restores you is an act of self-preservation and empowerment.

Prioritizing rest and care: Strength includes taking the time to nurture your body, mind, and spirit so that you can thrive, not just survive.

By letting go of the expectation to always be strong, you give yourself permission to be human. This shift doesn't diminish your resilience—it amplifies it, creating space for a life that honors both your challenges and your triumphs.

Redefining Strength: The Power of Vulnerability

True strength does not mean enduring everything alone; it means knowing when to lean on others, set boundaries, and care for yourself. Here's how to begin:

Acknowledge Your Humanity:

Remind yourself that you are allowed to feel tired, sad, or overwhelmed. These emotions do not make you weak—they make you human.

Embrace Vulnerability as Courage:

Allowing yourself to express fear, sadness, or frustration requires immense bravery. It opens the door to healing and deeper connections with others.

Ask for Help Without Shame:

Seeking support is not a sign of failure. It is a way to share the load and preserve your mental and physical health.

Exercises to Break Free

Challenge the Narrative:

- ✓ Write down the ways in which the Strong Black Woman archetype has shown up in your life

....

....

....

- ✓ Reflect on how these expectations have impacted your health, relationships, or sense of self.
- ✓ Practice Saying "No":
- ✓ Identify one responsibility or expectation you've taken on out of obligation rather than desire.
- ✓ Practice setting boundaries by saying no, and observe how it feels to prioritize yourself.

Create a Vulnerability List:

- ✓ Write down three people you trust enough to share your struggles with.

....

....

- ✓ Reach out to one of them this week and have an open, honest conversation about what you're feeling.

....

....

A New Definition of Strength

Strength is not about shouldering everything alone—it's about knowing your limits, valuing your well-being, and recognizing that vulnerability is a form of power. By breaking free from the Strong Black Woman archetype, you allow yourself the space to grow, heal, and connect authentically with yourself and others.

In the next chapter, we will explore how setting healthy boundaries can help you reclaim your time, energy, and emotional freedom.

Chapter 3: Power in Boundaries: Saying No Without Guilt

The ability to set boundaries is one of the most powerful tools for reclaiming your energy, emotional freedom, and sense of self. For many Black women, saying "no" can feel like a radical act in a world that expects them to be endlessly available, accommodating, and self-sacrificing. This chapter dives into the importance of boundaries, how to set them without guilt, and why they are essential for protecting your mental and emotional well-being.

Why Boundaries Are Hard to Set

Black women often face unique challenges when it comes to setting boundaries, shaped by societal expectations and cultural norms:

Cultural pressure to be "everything to everyone": The Strong Black Woman archetype often demands that you prioritize others over yourself, leaving little room for personal needs.

Fear of being labeled selfish or unkind: Saying "no" can bring feelings of guilt or fear of being judged harshly.

A history of being overlooked or undervalued: Sometimes, boundaries feel risky, as they challenge the fear of rejection or abandonment.

Understanding these barriers is the first step to dismantling them. You have the right to protect your time, energy, and emotional health without apology.

What Boundaries Look Like

Boundaries can be both emotional and practical. Here are a few examples:

Emotional boundaries:

- Saying no to people who drain your energy.
- Refusing to engage in conversations that make you uncomfortable or invalidate your feelings.

Practical boundaries:

- Setting limits on how much time you dedicate to others versus yourself.
- Communicating your availability clearly, whether at work, with family, or in relationships.

The Power of "No"

Learning to say "no" is a key aspect of reclaiming your power. Here's why:

- "No" is a Complete Sentence: You do not owe anyone a justification for prioritizing yourself.
- It Reaffirms Your Self-Worth: By setting limits, you demonstrate that your needs and time are valuable.
- It Creates Space for What Matters: Saying no to what doesn't serve you makes room for the things that truly align with your goals and well-being.

How to Set Boundaries Without Guilt

<u>Understand Your Limits:</u>

Reflect on the areas of your life where you feel overwhelmed or resentful. These are often places where boundaries are needed.

<u>Communicate Clearly and Kindly:</u>

Be direct and respectful when setting boundaries. For example, "I can't take on this task right now, but I appreciate you thinking of me."

<u>Practice Saying No:</u>

Start small by saying no to low-stakes requests. Build confidence over time as you see the positive impact of setting boundaries.

<u>Resist the Urge to Over-Explain:</u>

Avoid long justifications for your decisions. A simple, firm response is enough.

<u>Anticipate Pushback:</u>

Some people may not respect your boundaries immediately, especially if they've benefitted from you not having any. Stay firm and remind yourself that their reaction is not your responsibility.

Exercises for Setting Boundaries

Boundary Audit:

List areas in your life where you feel drained or taken advantage of.

....

....

....

....

....

....

Write one boundary you can implement for each area.

....

....

....

....

....

....

....

....

Practice Role-Playing:

Imagine scenarios where you need to set a boundary. Practice your response in front of a mirror or with a friend to build confidence.

Create a "Boundary Affirmation":

Write a statement to remind yourself of the importance of your boundaries, such as:

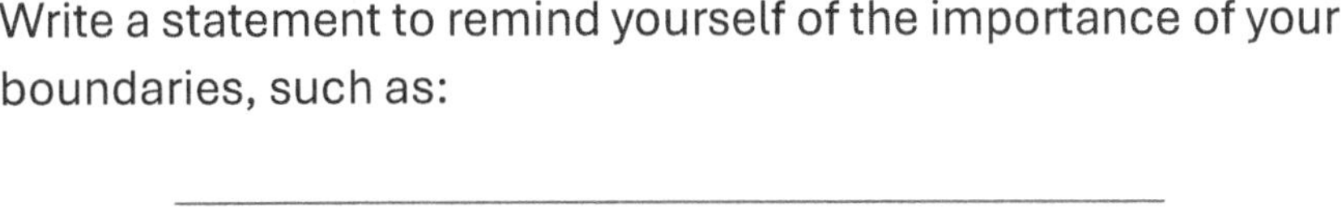

"I deserve to protect my energy,

and saying no is an act of self-respect."

Embracing the Freedom of Boundaries

Boundaries are not walls to keep others out; they are guidelines to show others how to treat you. By setting clear boundaries, you honor your worth, protect your well-being, and reclaim control over your life.

In the next chapter, we will explore how reclaiming your voice and breaking the silence can help you step into your authentic power.

Chapter 4: The Shadow of Silence: Finding Your Voice Again

Silence is not just the absence of words—it can be a reflection of deep fear, internalized oppression, or a learned response to trauma. For many Black women, silence has been a form of survival, born from navigating a world that often undervalues or misinterprets their voices. However, while silence might feel safe in the short term, it can create lasting wounds by stifling self-expression and diminishing your sense of agency.

This chapter delves into the roots of imposed silence, its impact on your well-being, and how to reclaim your voice with confidence and purpose. Because your voice—your truth—is not just powerful; it is necessary.

The Legacy of Silence

Black women's silence has often been enforced by societal pressures and cultural expectations. To understand the shadow of silence, we must examine where it originates:

Historical Roots:

In eras of slavery and segregation, Black women's voices were systematically silenced to maintain oppressive structures. Speaking up could mean punishment, ostracism, or worse. This history has left an imprint, teaching generations of women to equate silence with safety.

Cultural Norms:

Many Black women grow up with the belief that being "respectable" means not making waves. They are taught to avoid being "too loud" or "too confrontational," often to counteract harmful stereotypes like the "angry Black woman."

Personal Trauma:

Experiences of dismissal, ridicule, or rejection—whether in childhood, relationships, or the workplace—can reinforce the idea that staying silent is better than facing conflict or invalidation.

These layers of silence can lead to deep disconnection, not only from others but from yourself.

The Cost of Staying Silent

Silencing your voice may feel protective, but over time, it can cause harm. The consequences of silence can manifest in many ways:

Emotional Suppression:

When you hold back your feelings or opinions, you deny yourself the opportunity to process and release them. This suppression often leads to resentment, sadness, or even physical symptoms like fatigue and tension.

Erosion of Self-Worth:

Staying silent can send a subconscious message that your thoughts and needs don't matter, undermining your confidence and self-esteem.

Barriers to Authentic Relationships:

Silence creates walls, making it harder for others to truly know you. When you don't share your truth, you deny people the chance to connect with the real you.

<u>Missed Opportunities:</u>

By not speaking up, you may miss chances for growth, advocacy, or creating meaningful change in your personal and professional life.

Recognizing these costs is the first step toward breaking free from the shadow of silence.

Why Reclaiming Your Voice Matters

Your voice is more than just words—it is an extension of your identity and power. Reclaiming your voice allows you to:

<u>Express Your Truth:</u>

Speaking up lets you honor your experiences, values, and needs.

<u>Set Boundaries:</u>

When you use your voice, you communicate your limits and ensure others respect your space.

<u>Challenge Oppression:</u>

Sharing your perspective helps dismantle harmful narratives and creates space for other voices to rise.

<u>Empower Yourself:</u>

Every time you speak your truth, you reinforce your sense of self-worth and courage.

Steps to Reclaim Your Voice

Reclaiming your voice is not just about speaking up—it's about rediscovering the truth of who you are and allowing that truth to shape your interactions, decisions, and sense of self. It's a process that requires patience, self-compassion, and a willingness to confront fears and beliefs that have silenced you in the past.

Here, we'll delve deeply into the steps and practices that can help you reclaim your voice, amplify your confidence, and make self-expression an empowering, natural part of your daily life.

Acknowledge the Silence

The first step to reclaiming your voice is to recognize where and why you've silenced yourself. Silence can show up in various areas of your life:

At work: Perhaps you hesitate to share ideas in meetings for fear of being dismissed or judged.

In relationships: You might avoid expressing your feelings, fearing conflict or rejection.

Within your family: Long-standing dynamics may make it difficult to speak your truth without feeling misunderstood or criticized.

Reflect on the Why

Ask yourself these questions to better understand your silence:

- *What are the areas of my life where I feel voiceless?*

....

- *What am I afraid will happen if I speak up?*

....

- *Who taught me that silence was safer than expression?*

....

This step isn't about blaming yourself—it's about shining a light on the patterns and fears that have held you back. Acknowledging them is the first step toward breaking free.

Challenge Limiting Beliefs

Often, the fear of speaking up is rooted in beliefs that undermine your confidence or value. These beliefs may sound like:

"My opinion doesn't matter."

"If I speak up, I'll cause trouble or make things worse."

"I'm not good at expressing myself, so why bother?"

Replace Limiting Beliefs with Empowering Affirmations

To overcome these beliefs, consciously replace them with affirmations that reflect your worth and capabilities. For example:

Instead of: "My opinion doesn't matter," say: "My voice is valid and deserves to be heard."

Instead of: "I'll cause trouble if I speak up," say: "I can express myself with confidence and respect."

Instead of: "I'm not good at expressing myself," say: "With practice, I can share my thoughts clearly and effectively."

Write these affirmations in a journal, say them aloud in front of a mirror, or keep them as reminders on your phone or workspace. The more you reinforce these positive beliefs, the more they will begin to shape your mindset and actions.

Start Small

Reclaiming your voice doesn't mean diving into high-stakes situations right away. Confidence builds gradually, through small victories that show you it's safe to express yourself.

Practice in Low-Stakes Situations

Casual Conversations: Share your opinion on a topic during a lighthearted discussion with friends or colleagues.

Polite Disagreements: If someone says something you don't agree with, practice expressing your perspective respectfully. For example: *"I see it differently, and here's why."*

Ask for What You Want: Start with simple requests, like asking for help with a task or suggesting a movie you'd like to watch with a partner.

Each time you speak up, you reinforce the idea that your voice matters and that it's safe to express yourself.

Use "I" Statements

When reclaiming your voice, how you express yourself matters. Using "I" statements helps you communicate your feelings and needs without blaming or accusing others, which can reduce defensiveness and foster understanding.

Examples of "I" Statements

Instead of: "You never listen to me," say: "I feel unheard when I'm interrupted."

Instead of: "You're always late," say: "I feel disrespected when plans don't start on time."

By focusing on your own feelings and experiences, you create space for constructive conversations while asserting your perspective.

Find Your Medium

Speaking up doesn't always mean verbal communication. If expressing yourself aloud feels intimidating, consider other ways to reclaim your voice.

Alternative Mediums

Journaling: Write about your thoughts, feelings, and experiences. This can help you process emotions and clarify what you want to express.

Email or Text: If a face-to-face conversation feels overwhelming, start by expressing yourself through written communication.

Online Communities: Join supportive spaces where you can share your experiences anonymously or with like-minded individuals.

Finding the medium that feels most comfortable for you can make the process of reclaiming your voice feel more approachable.

Exercises to Strengthen Your Voice

The following exercises are designed to help you practice and reinforce your ability to express yourself with confidence and clarity.

1. Journaling Exercise

Write about a time when you silenced yourself. Reflect on:

What held you back in that moment?

....

....

....

What were you afraid might happen if you spoke up?

....

....

What would you say now if you could revisit that moment?

....

....

This exercise helps you identify patterns of silence and imagine alternative outcomes, building confidence for future situations.

2. Mirror Practice

Stand in front of a mirror and practice saying affirmations aloud, such as:

"I have the right to express myself."

"My voice matters, and it deserves to be heard."

"I speak with clarity and confidence."

Repeating these affirmations daily not only reinforces positive beliefs but also helps you get comfortable with hearing your own voice.

3. Speak Your Needs

Identify one thing you need in your personal or professional life. For example:

- At work, you might need more clarity on expectations for a project.
- At home, you might need more help with daily responsibilities.

....

....

....

....

....

Share this need with someone you trust, using "I" statements to communicate clearly and respectfully.

4. Storytelling Exercise

Write or record a story about a time when you overcame fear to speak your truth. Reflect on:

What motivated you to speak up?

....

....

....

How did it feel in the moment?

....

....

....

What was the outcome, and how did it empower you?

....

....

....

Revisiting these moments reminds you of your courage and reinforces your ability to advocate for yourself.

Building Confidence in Your Voice

Reclaiming your voice is not an overnight process—it's a journey that unfolds through practice, patience, and self-compassion. Each step forward, no matter how small, is a victory worth celebrating.

Tips for Building Confidence

Start Each Day with Affirmations: Remind yourself of your worth and your ability to speak your truth. Write here:

....

....

....

....

Reflect on Your Progress: Keep a journal of moments when you successfully expressed yourself, no matter how minor they may seem.

....

....

....

Seek Support: Surround yourself with people who value and encourage your self-expression. Write here their names:

....

....

Celebrate Your Wins: Acknowledge every instance where you used your voice, whether it was a simple comment or a meaningful conversation.

....

....

The Transformative Power of Reclaiming Your Voice

Reclaiming your voice isn't just about changing how others perceive you—it's about changing how you perceive yourself. Speaking your truth reinforces your self-worth, strengthens your relationships, and helps you live authentically.

Your voice is powerful, and the world needs to hear it. But more importantly, you need to hear it. Each time you speak up, you honor your journey, affirm your worth, and reclaim the space that has always been yours.

As you continue this journey, remember that your voice is a gift—one that has the power to transform not just your life but the lives of those around you.

In the next chapter, we'll explore how setting healthy boundaries can help you protect your energy, honor your needs, and create space for authentic self-expression.

Part 2: Heal Your Pain

Chapter 5: Tracing the Pain: Understanding Your Triggers

Emotional triggers can feel overwhelming and confusing.

A simple comment, action, or even a smell might provoke a reaction that seems out of proportion to the moment. These triggers are often the echoes of past experiences, a signal from your subconscious that something unresolved is surfacing. Understanding your triggers isn't just about managing them— it's about uncovering the deeper truths they reveal about your past, your emotions, and your needs.

In this chapter, we'll explore how to identify emotional triggers, connect them to their roots, and use them as a tool for healing rather than a source of distress.

What Are Emotional Triggers?

Emotional triggers are intense reactions that arise when something in your present environment evokes a memory or feeling tied to an unresolved past experience. Triggers act as windows into your subconscious, revealing wounds or fears that may have been buried over time. These reactions are often immediate, visceral, and can feel overwhelming. They might appear disproportionate to the current situation, but that's because they stem from deeper layers of your emotional history, often tied to pain or trauma that hasn't yet been fully processed or healed.

When triggered, you may experience a rush of emotions such as anger, sadness, fear, shame, or frustration. These emotions may surface suddenly, even in situations where others might not see a reason for such a strong response. It's important to remember that emotional triggers are not flaws or signs of weakness. Rather, they are your mind and body's way of alerting you to areas that need care, understanding, and healing.

Understanding the Roots of Triggers

Emotional triggers are shaped by your past experiences, particularly those that have left a significant emotional imprint. For many Black women, triggers are often rooted in societal and personal challenges that intersect with race, gender, and cultural expectations. These roots can stem from:

Past Trauma:

- Traumatic experiences, such as instances of abuse, neglect, or discrimination, can leave lasting emotional scars.
- When a current situation mirrors or reminds you of the original trauma, your emotional response is heightened as your mind tries to protect you from perceived harm.

Learned Responses:

- Growing up in environments where certain emotions were dismissed or invalidated can lead you to suppress your feelings.
- As an adult, when situations challenge these learned coping mechanisms, emotional triggers can emerge.

Generational Patterns:

Experiences of intergenerational trauma, particularly for Black women, can shape emotional responses. The weight of unspoken grief or inherited pain often manifests as heightened sensitivity to particular situations.

Common Triggers for Black Women

For Black women, emotional triggers are often deeply connected to the unique pressures and injustices faced both historically and in contemporary society. These triggers may arise from experiences that challenge your identity, boundaries, or sense of self-worth. Some common examples include:

Disrespect:

- Feeling dismissed, overlooked, or devalued in professional or personal settings can evoke anger or frustration.
- Examples might include being spoken over in meetings, having your contributions minimized, or being subjected to condescending attitudes.

Microaggressions:

- Microaggressions are subtle, often unintentional, comments or actions that demean or invalidate your identity.
- Examples include someone questioning your qualifications, making assumptions about your background, or commenting on your physical appearance in ways that feel invasive or objectifying.
- These moments can trigger feelings of invisibility or a need to constantly prove yourself.

Unfair Expectations:

- The societal expectation that Black women must always be "strong," capable of handling anything without showing vulnerability, is both unfair and harmful.
- When you feel pressured to meet these unrealistic standards, it can trigger feelings of exhaustion, resentment, and self-doubt.

Feelings of Abandonment:

- Experiences of rejection, lack of support, or being left to manage challenges on your own can trigger feelings of sadness and insecurity.
- This is especially true in relationships where you've been made to feel that your needs are secondary or unimportant.

The Emotional and Physical Impact of Triggers

When emotional triggers arise, they don't just affect your feelings—they can also manifest in physical ways. Your body often reacts instinctively to perceived emotional threats, activating the "fight, flight, or freeze" response. You might notice:

Physical Symptoms: Tightness in the chest, a racing heart, sweating, or a sense of agitation.

Cognitive Disruption: Difficulty concentrating, replaying the triggering event in your mind, or feeling stuck in negative thought patterns.

Behavioral Changes: Withdrawing from others, becoming defensive, or reacting impulsively.

These reactions are your body's way of protecting you, but they can feel exhausting and confusing, especially when you don't understand the root cause of the trigger.

Reframing Triggers as Signposts

It's important to shift your perspective on emotional triggers. While they can be uncomfortable and even painful, triggers are not your enemy. They are valuable signposts that point toward areas of your life that need attention, compassion, and healing. Each trigger reveals:

Unresolved Wounds: The areas where past pain continues to influence your present.

Boundaries in Need of Strengthening: Triggers often signal situations where your emotional or physical boundaries are being crossed.

Opportunities for Growth: By addressing what triggers you, you open the door to greater self-awareness, empowerment, and resilience.

Navigating Your Triggers

Dealing with triggers is not about suppressing or ignoring them—it's about understanding and managing them. Here are some initial steps to begin this process:

Recognize the Trigger:

Pay attention to moments when your emotions feel intense or out of proportion to the situation. Ask yourself: What just happened? How am I feeling?

Name the Emotion:

Give your feelings a name. Are you angry? Hurt? Scared? Naming your emotion helps you begin to understand and address it.

Identify the Source:

Reflect on what the current situation reminds you of. Is it similar to a past experience? What belief or fear might this trigger be tied to?

Practice Grounding Techniques:

When a trigger feels overwhelming, use grounding exercises like deep breathing, visualization, or physical movement to calm your body and regain a sense of control.

Why Understanding Triggers Matters

When you take the time to understand your triggers, you gain:

Clarity: You begin to recognize patterns in your emotions and reactions.

Control: Instead of being overwhelmed by your emotions, you can manage them more effectively.

Healing: Triggers often highlight unresolved wounds. Addressing these wounds helps you move forward with less emotional baggage.

Your triggers are not just about what's happening now—they're about the stories your mind and body have carried for years.

Steps to Identify and Understand Your Triggers

Pay Attention to Strong Reactions:

Notice moments when your emotions feel intense or out of proportion to the situation.

Ask yourself: What just happened? How did it make me feel?

....

....

....

Connect to the Past:

Reflect on whether this situation reminds you of something from your past.

For example:

If criticism at work feels devastating, could it be tied to childhood experiences of being judged or undervalued?

....

....

....

Explore the Deeper Emotion:

Triggers often mask deeper emotions like fear, insecurity, or sadness.

Ask yourself: What am I really feeling beneath this anger or frustration?

....

....

Identify Patterns:

Keep a journal of your triggers and your reactions. Over time, you'll begin to see patterns that reveal what consistently affects you.

Reflective Questions to Explore Hidden Emotions

To dig deeper into the roots of your triggers, consider the following questions:

What situation triggered me recently?

....

How did I react, and why did it feel so intense?

....

Does this remind me of a specific event, person, or relationship from my past?

....

What unspoken feelings or needs might be behind my reaction?

....

What would I say or do if I felt fully empowered in that moment?

....

These questions are not meant to judge your reactions but to help you better understand and validate them.

Exercises to Heal Through Understanding

The Trigger Journal:

Create a dedicated journal to document moments when you feel triggered. Include:

What happened.

....

How you felt.

....

What you think it connects to from your past.

....

The Inner Child Letter:

Write a letter to your younger self, addressing the pain or unmet needs that might be surfacing through your triggers.

For example: "I know you felt unseen and unheard as a child, but I see you now, and I'm here for you."

....

....

....

....

....

....

....

....

Reframing the Story:

Take a moment when you felt triggered and rewrite the narrative in a way that empowers you.

For instance, instead of viewing someone's dismissiveness as a reflection of your worth, see it as a reflection of their limitations, not yours.

....

....

....

....

....

....

....

Moving from Pain to Power

Triggers can feel like a loss of control, but they are actually an opportunity for transformation. By understanding and addressing them, you reclaim your power over your emotions and your life. Tracing the pain doesn't mean dwelling on it—it means acknowledging its source so you can begin to heal and move forward.

In the next chapter, we will explore how generational wounds contribute to emotional triggers and how breaking these cycles can lead to lasting healing.

Chapter 6: Healing Generational Wounds: Breaking the Cycle

Generational wounds, or intergenerational trauma, refer to patterns of pain, behaviors, and beliefs passed down through families. These wounds can manifest in various ways—emotional, mental, or even physical—and they often shape how we view ourselves, others, and the world. For Black women, these wounds are compounded by the historical weight of systemic oppression, racism, and cultural expectations.

This chapter will guide you in examining how generational trauma has influenced your life, and provide tools to break negative cycles, fostering healing for yourself and future generations.

What Are Generational Wounds?

Generational wounds are the unspoken stories and unresolved pain passed down through families. They can stem from:

Historical trauma: Experiences of slavery, segregation, or displacement, which have left scars on entire communities.

Family dynamics: Patterns like emotional neglect, unspoken grief, or a culture of silence about past hardships.

Cultural expectations: Pressure to conform to certain roles or behaviors, such as being "strong" or self-sacrificing.

These wounds are often perpetuated unconsciously, as coping mechanisms and survival strategies are handed down from one generation to the next.

How Generational Trauma Shapes Identity

Generational trauma, also known as intergenerational trauma, refers to the transmission of the effects of trauma from one generation to the next. This form of trauma often shapes identity in profound and subtle ways, influencing how individuals view themselves, interact with others, and navigate the world. For many Black women, generational trauma intersects with historical oppression, systemic racism, and cultural expectations, creating layers of complexity in how identity is formed and expressed.

This chapter delves into three key ways generational trauma shapes identity: the unspoken rules that govern family dynamics, the inherited fears and beliefs that influence behavior, and the cycles of pain that perpetuate harmful patterns. Understanding these elements is crucial to breaking free from their grip and reclaiming a more empowered and authentic sense of self.

Unspoken Rules: The Silent Architects of Identity

Every family develops a set of unspoken rules—norms and expectations that dictate how members interact, process emotions, and approach challenges. These rules are often born out of necessity, shaped by the family's history, cultural context, and collective experiences. While some unspoken rules provide structure and support, others can stifle emotional expression and personal growth, particularly when rooted in generational trauma.

The Legacy of Silence

In families affected by trauma, silence often becomes a survival mechanism. Painful events such as displacement, discrimination, or abuse may be too overwhelming or stigmatized to discuss openly. As a result, a rule of emotional suppression emerges:

"Don't talk about the past": Family members avoid discussing painful memories, believing that revisiting the trauma will only reopen wounds.

"Keep your emotions to yourself": Vulnerability is seen as a weakness, and expressing emotions like sadness or fear is discouraged.

"Always present a united front": Protecting the family's reputation or survival takes precedence over addressing individual needs or conflicts.

The Impact on Identity

These unspoken rules shape how individuals navigate their emotions and relationships:

- **Emotional Disconnection:**

When vulnerability is suppressed, individuals may struggle to identify and express their emotions. This disconnection can lead to feelings of isolation and difficulty forming deep, authentic relationships.

- **Internalized Shame:**

Avoiding discussions about painful memories can create a sense of shame around those experiences, even for individuals who weren't directly involved in the trauma.

- **Limited Self-Worth:**

Unspoken rules often emphasize external validation—such as academic or professional success—over intrinsic self-worth, leaving individuals feeling they must constantly prove their value.

Breaking free from the legacy of silence requires acknowledging these rules and consciously creating new ones that encourage open communication and emotional authenticity.

<u>Inherited Fears and Beliefs: The Emotional Echoes of Trauma</u>

Generational trauma doesn't just pass down stories or habits—it also transmits fears and beliefs that become deeply ingrained in family members' psyches. These fears often stem from historical or personal experiences of danger, injustice, or instability and are passed down as a way to protect future generations. However, they can also create barriers to living a fully empowered life.

The Origins of Inherited Fears

For Black women, inherited fears are often tied to systemic racism and cultural marginalization. Historical realities such as slavery, segregation, and ongoing discrimination have instilled messages of caution and hypervigilance, such as:

"You have to work twice as hard to be seen as equal": This belief reflects the reality of systemic bias but can create a relentless sense of pressure to achieve and overperform.

"Don't draw too much attention to yourself": Historically, visibility often meant vulnerability to harm, leading to a preference for staying under the radar.

"Trust is earned, not given": Experiences of betrayal or exploitation may foster a deep distrust of others, particularly those outside the family or community.

How These Fears Shape Identity

Inherited fears shape how individuals perceive themselves and navigate the world:

- **Perfectionism and Overwork:**

The belief that one must work harder than everyone else to succeed often leads to perfectionism, burnout, and difficulty celebrating achievements.

- **Hypervigilance:**

Constantly scanning for potential threats—whether emotional, social, or physical—can make it challenging to relax or fully engage in life.

- **Limited Risk-Taking:**

Fear of failure or judgment may prevent individuals from pursuing opportunities that align with their passions or dreams.

Challenging Inherited Beliefs

To break free from inherited fears, it's important to distinguish between beliefs that serve you and those that limit you. Ask yourself:

Is this belief rooted in my own experience, or is it something I've inherited?

....

Does this belief align with the life I want to create?

....

How can I reframe this belief in a way that empowers me?

....

For example, instead of internalizing the idea that you must work twice as hard, you might affirm: "I am capable and deserving of success on my own terms."

Cycles of Pain: Patterns That Perpetuate Trauma

Generational trauma often manifests in repeated behaviors and patterns that are passed down unconsciously. These cycles of pain are not born out of malice but from survival strategies developed by caregivers who were doing their best to navigate their own wounds.

Common Cycles of Pain

- *Avoiding Emotional Intimacy:*

Families affected by trauma may struggle to build emotionally open relationships, leading to distant or strained connections.

For example, a parent who suppresses their own emotions may unintentionally teach their child to do the same.

- *Normalizing Overwork:*

Overworking as a means of survival or coping can become a family norm, leaving little room for rest or self-care.

This cycle can perpetuate the belief that worth is tied to productivity rather than inherent value.

- *Suppressing Anger:*

In families where anger was met with punishment or fear, individuals may learn to suppress their anger rather than express it constructively.

Over time, suppressed anger can lead to resentment, burnout, or even physical health issues.

Recognizing the Patterns

Breaking these cycles begins with awareness. Reflect on the following questions:

What behaviors or patterns have I inherited from my family?

....

How do these patterns affect my relationships, emotions, and self-image?

....

What would I like to do differently for myself and future generations?

....

Breaking Free from Generational Trauma

Breaking free from generational trauma is not about rejecting your family or heritage—it's about honoring your past while consciously creating a new path forward. Here are some strategies to help you navigate this process:

- **Acknowledge the Pain:**

Name the patterns, fears, and unspoken rules that have shaped your identity. Understanding their origins can help you approach them with compassion rather than judgment.

....

....

- **Seek Support:**

Healing from generational trauma is a complex process that often benefits from external support, such as therapy, support groups, or trusted mentors.

- **Create New Narratives:**

Replace inherited beliefs with affirmations and values that align with the life you want to build. For example:

Instead of: "Vulnerability is weakness," affirm: "Vulnerability is a source of strength and connection."

....

....

- **Model Healthy Behaviors:**

By setting boundaries, prioritizing self-care, and practicing emotional expression, you can model healthier patterns for future generations.

- **Reconnect with Joy:**

Trauma often focuses on survival at the expense of joy. Intentionally seek out activities, relationships, and experiences that bring you happiness and fulfillment.

Generational trauma is a powerful force, but it does not have to define you. By recognizing its impact on your identity and taking intentional steps to break harmful patterns, you reclaim your power and create space for healing, growth, and authenticity.

The work you do today not only transforms your own life but also paves the way for future generations to inherit a legacy of resilience, self-love, and freedom. In breaking the cycles of pain, you become the bridge between the past and a brighter, more empowered future.

Breaking the Cycle

Healing generational wounds doesn't mean blaming past generations—it means acknowledging the pain they carried and choosing a new path forward. Here are some steps to start breaking the cycle:

Understand the Source:

Reflect on your family's history. What struggles, traumas, or challenges have shaped your family's story?

....

....

....

....

....

Ask yourself: What patterns do I see in how emotions are handled, how conflict is resolved, or how success is defined?

....

....

Practice Compassion:

Recognize that previous generations often did the best they could with the resources and knowledge available to them.

Show compassion for their pain, even as you commit to doing things differently.

....

Release What No Longer Serves You:

Identify beliefs or behaviors that you've inherited but no longer want to carry.

For example, if your family normalized suppressing emotions, you can choose to prioritize emotional expression and validation.

....

Set Intentional Boundaries:

Breaking cycles often requires setting boundaries with family members who may not understand or support your healing journey.

Communicate your needs clearly, such as: "I love you, but I can't take on this role anymore."

....

....

Model New Behaviors:

Be the change you want to see for future generations. Show others that it's possible to address pain, seek help, and prioritize well-being.

Tools for Healing Generational Wounds

Journaling the Family Narrative:

Write about your family's story, focusing on the challenges and strengths passed down.

Reflect on what you want to honor and what you want to let go of.

....

....

....

....

....

....

....

....

....

....

....

....

Meditation for Ancestral Healing

Ancestral healing meditation is a deeply spiritual and grounding practice that allows you to connect with your lineage, honor the sacrifices of those who came before you, and draw on their strength as you continue your journey of healing. This meditation offers an opportunity to acknowledge the pain and resilience carried through generations, while also inviting blessings and guidance from your ancestors to help you break harmful cycles and create a path of freedom and empowerment.

The Purpose of Ancestral Healing Meditation

The practice of ancestral healing meditation helps you:

- ***Acknowledge the past:*** Recognize the pain, struggles, and sacrifices that your ancestors endured.
- ***Cultivate gratitude:*** Honor the resilience and strength they passed down to you.
- ***Seek guidance:*** Open yourself to the wisdom and blessings of your ancestors as you navigate your own healing journey.
- ***Release generational pain:*** Offer compassion to past wounds and visualize breaking cycles of trauma.

This meditation is a sacred act of love and connection, bridging the gap between your past and present while empowering you to create a brighter future.

Preparing for the Meditation

- Find a Quiet Space:

Choose a comfortable, peaceful environment where you won't be disturbed.

You may want to light a candle or burn incense as a symbol of calling your ancestors into the space.

- Set an Intention:

Before beginning, take a moment to reflect on your intention for this meditation. You might silently say:

"I honor my ancestors and seek their wisdom and strength for my healing."

"I release the pain of the past and invite blessings for my future."

....

....

....

....

....

- Gather Meaningful Items (Optional):

If possible, include objects that represent your ancestry, such as family photos, heirlooms, or symbols of your cultural heritage. These can help you feel more connected during the meditation.

Step-by-Step Guide to Ancestral Healing Meditation

- Ground Yourself:

Sit comfortably with your feet flat on the floor or in a cross-legged position. Close your eyes and take a deep breath in through your nose, holding it for a moment, and then exhale slowly through your mouth.

Repeat this deep breathing for a few moments, focusing on the sensation of the air filling and leaving your lungs.

- Visualize a Sacred Space:

Picture yourself in a serene and sacred environment, such as a lush forest, a tranquil beach, or a beautiful garden. This is a safe space where you will meet your ancestors.

- Call Upon Your Ancestors:

Silently or aloud, invite your ancestors into this sacred space. You might say:

"I welcome the ancestors who love me, guide me, and wish me healing and peace. Known and unknown, I honor your presence."

Imagine their energy filling the space, surrounding you with warmth and love.

- Meet Your Ancestors:

Visualize your ancestors appearing one by one or as a collective group. They may take familiar forms—faces you've seen in photos or people you've heard about in stories—or appear as an abstract sense of energy or light.

Feel their presence and the strength of the lineage that connects you to them.

- Offer Gratitude and Compassion:

In your mind, speak directly to your ancestors, expressing gratitude for their sacrifices, resilience, and the life they made possible for you. You might say:

"Thank you for your strength, for your endurance, and for paving the way for me to be here today."

- Acknowledge their pain or struggles with compassion:

"I see the challenges you faced, and I honor your courage in the face of adversity."

- Receive Their Blessings:

Imagine your ancestors extending their hands or surrounding you with light. Feel their love, guidance, and blessings pouring into you, offering you the strength to break cycles of pain and create new, healthy patterns.

- You might silently hear or feel their encouragement, such as:

"You are strong, and you are not alone."

"We are with you on this journey."

- Visualize Breaking Cycles:

Picture the pain, fear, or trauma passed down through generations as a chain connecting you to the past.

Visualize yourself gently breaking the chain, replacing it with a golden thread of love, healing, and resilience that connects you to your ancestors and future generations.

- Offer a Closing Gesture:

Thank your ancestors for their presence and blessings. You might say:

"I am grateful for your love and guidance. I carry your strength with me as I walk my path."

Imagine them slowly retreating, leaving you with a sense of peace and empowerment.

- Return to the Present:

Bring your awareness back to your breath, inhaling deeply and exhaling slowly. Wiggle your fingers and toes to ground yourself.

Open your eyes when you're ready, carrying the warmth and connection of the meditation with you.

Reflections After the Meditation

After completing the meditation, take a few moments to reflect on the experience. You might want to:

- **Journal**: Write about any images, feelings, or messages that came up during the meditation.

- **Draw or Create**: Use art or other creative outlets to express your connection to your ancestors and the healing you experienced.
- **Repeat Affirmations**: Affirm the strength and guidance you received with statements like:

"I am supported by the love and wisdom of my ancestors."

"I carry their resilience and create new patterns of healing and joy."

When to Use Ancestral Healing Meditation

This meditation can be practiced whenever you:

- Feel disconnected from your roots or identity.
- Need strength and guidance during challenging times.
- Want to honor your ancestors and their contributions to your life.
- Are working through generational trauma and seeking closure or peace.

Final Thoughts

Ancestral healing meditation is a sacred practice that connects you to a lineage of strength, wisdom, and love. It reminds you that you are not alone in your journey of healing and transformation—your ancestors are with you, supporting and guiding you every step of the way.

As you continue to heal and grow, this practice can serve as a powerful reminder of the resilience and courage you've inherited, empowering you to break cycles of pain and create a legacy of empowerment for future generations.

Create a Family Healing Ritual:

Family healing rituals are powerful practices that bring intention and meaning to the journey of releasing generational pain, fostering connection, and committing to growth. These rituals can be as simple or elaborate as you wish, but their purpose remains the same: to create a sacred space where you and your loved ones can honor the past, release what no longer serves you, and build a foundation for a healthier future.

This section provides ideas and guidance for creating a family healing ritual that reflects your unique values, culture, and needs. Whether done individually or collectively, these rituals serve as a symbolic and tangible way to acknowledge pain, celebrate resilience, and embrace transformation.

Why Create a Family Healing Ritual?

A family healing ritual can help:

Acknowledge the Past: It provides an opportunity to openly recognize the pain, patterns, or behaviors that have shaped your family dynamics.

Symbolize Release: By performing intentional actions, such as burning or discarding objects, you create a physical and emotional sense of letting go.

Foster Connection: Engaging in a shared ritual can strengthen bonds within the family, creating a sense of unity and shared purpose.

Commit to Growth: Rituals mark a transition point, signaling your dedication to creating healthier patterns for yourself and future generations.

Planning Your Family Healing Ritual

Creating a meaningful ritual involves thoughtful preparation. Here's how to get started:

1. **Set an Intention:**

Reflect on what you hope to achieve through the ritual. Your intention might include:

- Releasing inherited patterns or beliefs that no longer serve you.
- Honoring family resilience and strength.
- Committing to new ways of relating to one another.

Example: "We release the pain of the past and embrace a future filled with love, understanding, and healing."

2. **Choose a Sacred Space:**

Select a location where you feel comfortable and connected. This could be your living room, a backyard, or a special place in nature.

Decorate the space with meaningful items such as candles, flowers, family photos, or cultural symbols.

3. **Gather Supplies:**

Depending on your ritual, you may need items such as:

- Candles for lighting and setting intentions.
- Paper and pens for writing down thoughts or patterns to release.
- A bowl or fireproof container for safely burning paper.
- Objects that represent your family's heritage or values.

Ritual Ideas for Healing and Growth

Here are some examples of family healing rituals you can adapt to your needs:

1. Burning Ceremony for Release

Purpose: To let go of generational patterns, pain, or limiting beliefs.

How to Perform:

- Each family member writes down a pattern, fear, or behavior they want to release on a piece of paper.

Example: "I release the fear of failure that has held me back."

- Take turns sharing what you've written (if comfortable) and placing the paper in a fireproof container.
- Light the papers on fire, watching as the flames consume them.
- As the smoke rises, imagine the pain or pattern leaving your family's collective energy.
- Close the ritual with a moment of gratitude for the courage to let go.

2. Candlelight Ceremony for Intention-Setting

Purpose: To symbolize light, hope, and new beginnings for the family.

How to Perform:

- Gather in a circle, and give each person a candle.
- Light one central candle, representing your family's shared strength and unity.

- Pass the flame from the central candle to each family member's candle. As each person lights their candle, they state an intention for growth or healing.

Example: "I commit to practicing patience and understanding in our relationships."

- Allow the candles to burn as you sit together in silence or share positive memories and hopes for the future.

3. Creating a Family Manifesto

Purpose: To collectively define the values, behaviors, and beliefs that will guide your family moving forward.

How to Perform:

- As a group, discuss patterns or behaviors you want to leave behind, such as avoidance, criticism, or overwork.
- Brainstorm new values and commitments you'd like to embrace, such as open communication, mutual support, or celebrating successes.
- Write these values and commitments into a "Family Manifesto."

Example: "We commit to speaking with kindness, supporting each other's dreams, and creating space for rest and self-care."

- Display the manifesto in a shared space as a reminder of your collective intentions.

4. Ancestral Honoring Ritual

Purpose: To connect with and honor the strength and sacrifices of your ancestors.

How to Perform:

- Create an altar with photos, heirlooms, or symbols representing your ancestry.
- Light a candle and invite the presence of your ancestors, saying:

"We honor the ancestors who came before us. Your strength and resilience live within us."

- Each family member shares a gratitude or reflection about their connection to the past.
- Conclude by affirming your commitment to carrying their strength forward into a healthier future.

5. Planting Seeds for Growth

Purpose: To symbolize new beginnings and growth within the family.

How to Perform:

- Gather seeds or small plants, along with a pot or space in a garden.
- Each family member plants a seed, stating an intention or hope for the family's future as they do so.

Example: "I plant this seed for a future filled with love and understanding."

- Tend to the plants together as a reminder of your shared commitment to growth.

Tips for a Meaningful Ritual

Personalize the Ritual:

Incorporate cultural or spiritual elements that resonate with your family, such as prayers, songs, or traditional practices.

Encourage Openness:

Create a safe space for everyone to express themselves without judgment. Participation should be voluntary, and no one should feel pressured to share more than they're comfortable with.

Focus on Positivity:

While it's important to acknowledge pain, emphasize hope, resilience, and the opportunities for growth.

Follow Up:

After the ritual, check in with family members to discuss how they're feeling and any insights they gained. Consider making the ritual an annual or seasonal tradition to reinforce its impact.

The Power of Ritual in Family Healing

Family healing rituals are more than symbolic gestures—they are acts of intention that create space for change. They help you process emotions, foster connection, and reinforce the values you want to carry forward.

By committing to a shared ritual, you and your family signal a collective dedication to breaking cycles of pain and building a legacy of love, understanding, and resilience. Whether performed once or repeated regularly, these rituals become meaningful milestones on the journey toward healing and growth.

Affirmations for Breaking Cycles:

Repeat affirmations like:

"I honor the strength of my ancestors, but I am not bound by their pain."

"I have the power to create a new legacy of healing and love."

A Healthier Future

Breaking generational cycles is not just about healing your own pain—it's about creating a ripple effect for those who come after you. As you heal, you teach others—your children, nieces, nephews, or even friends—that they, too, can choose a different path.

You are not defined by the pain you've inherited. By doing the work to heal, you create space for joy, freedom, and wholeness in your life and the lives of those around you.

In the next chapter, we will explore how meditation can be used as a powerful tool to calm the mind, process emotions, and guide you on your healing journey.

Chapter 7: Meditation as Medicine: A Path to Inner Peace

Meditation is a powerful practice for calming the mind, reconnecting with your inner self, and creating space for healing. For Black women, meditation can be especially transformative—a tool to silence the external noise, reclaim your personal power, and address the emotions that have been buried or overlooked. This chapter introduces simple meditation techniques to help you navigate anger, process pain, and explore forgiveness, while offering practical guidance for incorporating meditation into your daily life.

Why Meditation Matters

Meditation is more than just sitting in silence; it's a practice of intentional awareness that allows you to tune into your thoughts and emotions without judgment. For centuries, meditation has been used to:

Calm the mind: By focusing on the present moment, meditation reduces stress and anxiety.

Process emotions: It provides a safe space to acknowledge and release difficult feelings.

Reconnect with your inner self: Meditation fosters a deeper understanding of your thoughts, needs, and desires.

Cultivate resilience: Regular practice helps you respond to challenges with greater clarity and strength.

For Black women, who often face societal pressures, microaggressions, and the burden of historical trauma, meditation offers a sanctuary—a place to breathe, reflect, and heal.

Preparing for Meditation

Before you begin, create a space that feels calming and supportive:

Find a Quiet Space: Choose a place where you won't be disturbed, even if it's just a corner of your home.

Set the Mood: Light a candle, play soft music, or incorporate essential oils like lavender to create a soothing atmosphere.

Sit Comfortably: You can sit on a chair, cushion, or even lie down—just make sure your posture allows you to relax without falling asleep.

Set an Intention: Decide what you want to focus on during your meditation, such as letting go of anger or cultivating self-love.

Simple Meditation Techniques

The Breath Anchor:

- Sit comfortably and close your eyes.
- Focus on your breath as it enters and leaves your nose.
- When your mind wanders (which is natural), gently bring your focus back to your breath.
- Practice this for 5–10 minutes to center your mind.

Body Scan Meditation:

- Lie down or sit in a relaxed position.
- Bring your attention to your feet and slowly move up through your body, noticing any tension or sensations.
- Imagine releasing tension with each exhale.
- This practice helps you connect with your body and release physical stress.

Visualization Meditation:

- Picture a safe, peaceful place—perhaps a beach, forest, or quiet room.
- Imagine yourself surrounded by warmth, love, and acceptance.
- Use this space to reflect on a challenging emotion, allowing it to surface without judgment.

Guided Meditations for Anger, Pain, and Forgiveness

For Anger:

- Sit comfortably and take a few deep breaths.
- Imagine your anger as a flame inside you. Visualize it burning brightly but safely, contained in a lantern.
- With each breath, imagine the flame softening, its heat turning into warmth that empowers you rather than consumes you.

For Pain:

- Close your eyes and place your hand over your heart.

- Breathe deeply and silently repeat: "It's okay to feel this pain. I am safe."
- Imagine your breath flowing to the area where you feel the pain, creating space for healing.

For Forgiveness:

- Picture the person you want to forgive—or yourself—standing in front of you.
- Silently say: "*I release the hold this pain has on me. I choose freedom.*"
- Visualize a light surrounding both of you, symbolizing the release of resentment.

Incorporating Meditation into Daily Life

Meditation doesn't have to be a lengthy or formal practice. Here's how to weave it into your routine:

Morning Mindfulness: Start your day with 5 minutes of focused breathing to set a calm tone.

Midday Reset: Take a short break to close your eyes and focus on your breath, especially during stressful moments.

Evening Reflection: Before bed, meditate on what went well during the day and what you'd like to release.

You can also pair meditation with other self-care practices, such as journaling, yoga, or prayer, to enhance its effects.

The Power of Consistency

Meditation is like a muscle—the more you practice, the stronger your ability to find peace and clarity becomes. Start small, with just a few minutes a day, and build from there. Over time, you'll notice a greater sense of calm, resilience, and self-awareness.

Final Thoughts

Meditation is both a refuge and a tool for transformation. It allows you to sit with your emotions, honor your experiences, and reconnect with the deepest parts of yourself. As you continue this journey of healing and self-discovery, meditation can serve as a reminder that peace is always within reach, no matter what storms may come.

In the next chapter, we'll explore the transformative power of forgiveness—not as an obligation, but as a gift you give yourself on the path to freedom.

Chapter 8: The Power of Forgiveness: For Others and Yourself

Forgiveness is one of the most misunderstood concepts on the path to healing. Many believe forgiveness is about excusing those who have hurt us or pretending the pain didn't happen. In reality, forgiveness is not for the person who caused the harm—it's a gift to yourself. It's a way to release resentment, reclaim your emotional freedom, and free yourself from the weight of the past.

In this chapter, we'll explore what forgiveness truly means, why it's a powerful act of self-love, and how to begin the process of letting go.

Redefining Forgiveness

Forgiveness is often seen as a passive act, but it's one of the most active and courageous steps you can take in your healing journey. Here's what forgiveness is—and isn't:

Forgiveness Is Not:

- Approval of Harm: Forgiving someone doesn't mean what they did was okay.
- Reconciliation: You can forgive someone without reestablishing a relationship with them.
- Forgetting: Forgiveness doesn't erase the memory of the hurt—it transforms how you carry it.

Forgiveness Is:

- A Gift to Yourself: Letting go of resentment frees you from being emotionally tied to the person or event that hurt you.
- A Step Toward Freedom: Holding onto anger or pain often keeps you stuck. Forgiveness allows you to move forward.
- An Act of Strength: It takes courage and self-awareness to forgive, especially when the hurt runs deep.

Why Forgiveness Matters

Refusing to forgive can feel like protection—holding onto anger can seem like a way to shield yourself from future harm. But resentment often hurts you more than the person who caused the pain.

The Emotional Cost of Resentment:

- Resentment and anger can lead to stress, anxiety, and even physical ailments like headaches or muscle tension.
- Carrying unresolved pain drains your energy, leaving less room for joy and growth.

The Freedom of Forgiveness:

- Forgiveness helps you break free from the emotional chains of the past.
- It allows you to reclaim your power and focus on what truly matters—your healing and happiness.

Forgiveness for Yourself

While forgiving others is important, self-forgiveness is equally vital. Many of us carry guilt, shame, or regret for mistakes we've made or ways we've handled painful situations. Forgiving yourself is a necessary step toward self-compassion and growth.

Letting Go of Self-Judgment:

- Acknowledge that you are human and that imperfection is part of the journey.
- Remind yourself that every mistake is an opportunity for learning and growth.

Embracing Your Own Healing:

Self-forgiveness creates space for self-love. It's a way to release the heavy burden of shame and allow yourself to heal fully.

Steps to Begin Forgiveness

Acknowledge the Pain:

Name the person or situation that hurt you. Be honest about the impact it has had on your emotions, relationships, and sense of self.

....

....

....

Understand Your Emotions:

Reflect on the anger, sadness, or betrayal you feel. What does holding onto these emotions cost you?

....

....

....

....

Decide to Forgive:

Forgiveness doesn't happen overnight—it's a choice you make repeatedly. Start by deciding that you are ready to begin the process, even if it feels difficult.

....

....

....

Separate the Person from the Pain:

Recognize that the person who hurt you is flawed and human, just like you. This doesn't excuse their actions but helps you let go of their power over your emotions.

....

....

Release the Burden:

Imagine physically letting go of the resentment, whether through visualization, writing, or a symbolic act (like burning a letter or releasing a stone).

....

Exercises to Practice Forgiveness

Write a Forgiveness Letter:

Write a letter to the person who hurt you. Pour out your emotions—anger, sadness, and everything in between.

End the letter with a statement of release, such as: "I release the hold this pain has on me. I choose peace."

You don't need to send the letter; the act of writing is for your healing.

Guided Visualization:

Sit in a quiet place and close your eyes. Picture the person who hurt you (or yourself, if practicing self-forgiveness).

Imagine a cord connecting you to them, representing the pain and resentment. Visualize cutting the cord and watching it dissolve, freeing both of you.

Daily Forgiveness Affirmations:

Repeat affirmations to help shift your mindset, such as:

- ✓ "I am free from the pain of the past."
- ✓ "Forgiveness is a gift I give myself."
- ✓ "I release resentment and embrace peace."

Release Ritual:

Write the name of the person or situation you want to forgive on a piece of paper.

Burn it, shred it, or bury it as a symbolic act of letting go.

Moving Forward

Forgiveness doesn't mean you'll never feel pain or anger about what happened—it means those emotions no longer control you. It's a process, not a one-time act, and it takes time and self-compassion.

By forgiving others and yourself, you create space for healing, joy, and freedom. You reclaim the energy that resentment once consumed and redirect it toward your growth and happiness.

In the next chapter, we will explore how to celebrate your progress and integrate practices that honor your healing journey through sacred self-care.

Part 3: Celebrate Your True Self

Chapter 9: Sacred Self-Care: Restoring Balance in Mind, Body, and Spirit

Self-care is often misunderstood as indulgence or luxury. However, sacred self-care goes beyond the surface—it's an intentional practice of nurturing your soul, honoring your needs, and restoring balance in your life. For Black women, self-care can be a radical and healing act, especially in a world that often demands your energy while neglecting your well-being.

This chapter explores daily practices for authentic self-care and rituals that celebrate your body, mind, and spirit, helping you reconnect with your true self and find peace and joy.

What Is Sacred Self-Care?

Sacred self-care is rooted in mindfulness, intentionality, and self-love. It's about creating routines and moments that prioritize your mental, physical, and emotional health, treating your well-being as a sacred priority rather than an afterthought.

Sacred self-care means:

- ✓ *Listening to Your Needs:* Tuning into your mind and body to understand what you need to feel whole and balanced.
- ✓ *Honoring Your Energy:* Recognizing your limits and creating space for rest and renewal.
- ✓ *Celebrating Yourself:* Viewing self-care not as selfish but as an act of honoring your worth.

Why Self-Care Is Essential

For Black women, self-care is not just about relaxation—it's an act of survival and resistance.

- ✓ *Combatting Burnout:* Constantly navigating the pressures of life, work, family, and societal expectations can leave you depleted. Self-care restores your energy.
- ✓ *Breaking Generational Patterns:* Prioritizing your well-being teaches future generations the value of self-love and balance.
- ✓ *Reconnecting with Joy:* Self-care allows you to step away from stress and reconnect with the simple pleasures of life.

Daily Practices for Authentic Self-Care

Sacred self-care doesn't require grand gestures. Small, consistent actions can make a big difference in restoring balance and nurturing your soul.

Morning Rituals: Starting Your Day with Intention

How you begin your day sets the tone for everything that follows. A thoughtful and intentional morning ritual helps you ground yourself, cultivate positivity, and create a sense of purpose before the demands of the day take over. Morning rituals don't have to be lengthy or elaborate; even a few mindful practices can profoundly impact your mental, emotional, and physical well-being.

This section provides a detailed exploration of morning rituals, offering ideas and strategies to help you craft a routine that energizes your body, focuses your mind, and nourishes your spirit.

Why Morning Rituals Matter

Starting your day with intention offers several benefits:

- ✓ *Mental Clarity:* By pausing to center yourself, you can approach the day with focus and calm rather than stress or overwhelm.
- ✓ *Emotional Resilience:* Morning rituals provide space to connect with gratitude, set intentions, and foster positivity, helping you respond to challenges with a balanced mindset.
- ✓ *Physical Energy:* Gentle movement or breathwork in the morning awakens your body, improving circulation, flexibility, and vitality.
- ✓ *Sense of Control:* Morning rituals are an act of self-care that remind you to prioritize your needs and goals before the demands of the outside world.

Creating a Morning Ritual

Your morning ritual should reflect your unique needs, values, and schedule. Here's how to create a practice that works for you:

1. **Set the Environment:**
   - ✓ Choose a peaceful space where you feel comfortable and relaxed.
   - ✓ If possible, add items that inspire you, such as a candle, a journal, or a favorite piece of artwork.

2. **Keep It Manageable:**
   - ✓ Start small with just one or two practices and gradually build your routine. Even 5–10 minutes can make a difference.
3. **Be Consistent:**
   - ✓ Aim to practice your morning ritual at the same time each day to build a habit. Consistency helps create a sense of stability and structure.

Morning Ritual Ideas

Here are some practices to consider incorporating into your routine:

1. Meditation or Deep Breathing

Why: Meditation and breathwork calm your mind, reduce stress, and help you feel centered.

- ✓ How to Practice:
- • Sit comfortably in a quiet space and close your eyes.
- • Take slow, deep breaths, inhaling for a count of four, holding for four, and exhaling for six. Repeat this for 2–5 minutes.

If you prefer guided meditation, use an app or listen to a recording that aligns with your intentions, such as cultivating gratitude or releasing anxiety.

Tip: If you're new to meditation, start with just one minute and gradually extend the duration as you become more comfortable.

2. Gratitude Journaling

Why: Gratitude shifts your focus from what's missing to what's present, fostering positivity and contentment.

- ✓ How to Practice:
- Keep a journal by your bed or in your morning space.
- Write down one to three things you're grateful for each morning. These can be simple (a good night's sleep) or profound (a meaningful conversation with a loved one).
- Reflect on why these things matter to you and how they enrich your life.

Tip: If you struggle to think of something, start with basic comforts like shelter, food, or the ability to start a new day.

3. Stretching or Gentle Movement

Why: Stretching awakens your body, improves flexibility, and releases tension accumulated during sleep.

- ✓ How to Practice:
- Spend 5–10 minutes performing gentle stretches, focusing on areas like your neck, shoulders, back, and legs.
- Consider incorporating yoga poses such as Child's Pose, Cat-Cow, or Downward Dog to enhance your practice.
- Pair your movements with deep breaths, inhaling as you stretch and exhaling as you release.

Tip: If you enjoy music, play calming or uplifting tunes to make the experience more enjoyable.

4. Set an Intention for the Day

Why: Setting an intention gives your day focus and purpose, helping you align your actions with your values.

- ✓ How to Practice:
- Take a moment to reflect on what you want to prioritize for the day.
- State your intention as a positive affirmation, such as:

"Today, I will approach challenges with patience and grace."

"I choose to focus on progress, not perfection."

- Write your intention in your journal or repeat it silently throughout the day.

Tip: Revisit your intention during moments of stress or uncertainty to regain focus.

5. Hydrate and Nourish Your Body

Why: Drinking water and eating a nutritious breakfast replenish your energy and support your overall health.

- ✓ How to Practice:
- Start your morning with a glass of water, perhaps adding a slice of lemon for a refreshing boost.
- Choose a breakfast that fuels you, such as oatmeal with fruit, a smoothie, or eggs with whole-grain toast.
- Eat mindfully, savoring each bite and avoiding distractions like your phone or TV.

Tip: Prep your breakfast the night before if you're short on time in the morning.

6. Visualization Exercise

Why: Visualization helps you mentally rehearse success and boost confidence in achieving your goals.

- ✓ How to Practice:
- Sit comfortably and close your eyes.
- Picture yourself moving through your day with ease and confidence. Visualize completing tasks, handling challenges gracefully, and ending the day feeling accomplished.
- Notice the emotions associated with this vision, such as pride, joy, or peace, and allow them to motivate you.

Tip: Pair visualization with affirmations to reinforce positive outcomes.

7. Inspirational Reading or Listening

Why: Consuming uplifting content in the morning can inspire and energize you for the day ahead.

- ✓ How to Practice:
- Read a passage from a motivational book, devotional, or poem that resonates with you.
- Alternatively, listen to a short podcast or audio recording that aligns with your goals or interests.
- Reflect on how the message applies to your life and how you can carry it into your day.

Tip: Keep your reading or listening material accessible so it's easy to incorporate into your routine.

Combining Rituals for a Customized Routine

Your morning ritual doesn't have to include every practice listed here. Choose a combination that feels meaningful and manageable for you. For example:

- **10-Minute Routine:** Start with deep breathing (2 minutes), journal one gratitude (3 minutes), and stretch (5 minutes).
- **30-Minute Routine:** Add a visualization exercise (10 minutes) and inspirational reading (10 minutes) to the shorter routine.
- **Flexible Routine:** Rotate practices depending on your needs and schedule, focusing on what brings you the most benefit each day.

Sticking to Your Morning Ritual

Prepare the Night Before:

- Lay out your journal, set your alarm, and create a calming environment to make your morning routine seamless.

Be Consistent but Flexible:

- Aim to practice your ritual regularly, but allow for adjustments if life gets busy.

Celebrate Progress:

- Acknowledge the positive changes you notice, such as increased energy, focus, or emotional balance.

Final Thoughts

A morning ritual is more than a series of tasks—it's a commitment to starting your day with intention, care, and purpose. By dedicating even a few minutes to practices that nourish your mind, body, and spirit, you set a powerful tone for the day ahead.

Remember, your ritual is for you. Adapt it as needed, and let it be a source of grounding, inspiration, and joy that supports your well-being and growth every day.

Mindful Movement:

Choose activities that feel good for your body, such as yoga, dancing, walking, or anything that allows you to move with joy and purpose.

Nourishing Your Body:

Make mindful food choices that fuel and energize you. Enjoy meals without distractions, focusing on the textures and flavors.

Midday Pauses:

Take breaks during your day to check in with yourself. Ask:

How am I feeling? What do I need right now?

Evening Wind-Downs:

Create a calming nighttime routine, such as:

- A warm bath with essential oils.
- Reading a book or journaling about your day.
- Listening to soothing music or practicing gratitude before bed.

Rituals to Honor Your Body, Mind, and Spirit

Sacred self-care rituals can deepen your connection to yourself and help you celebrate your journey.

Body Rituals:

Self-Massage: Use oils or lotions to gently massage your hands, feet, or body, thanking each part for its strength and support.

Detox Baths: Create a ritual bath with Epsom salts, herbs, or flowers. Light candles and focus on releasing tension as you soak.

Mind Rituals:

Gratitude Practice: Write down three things you're grateful for each day. This shifts your focus from stress to abundance.

Affirmations: Start or end your day with positive affirmations like:

"I am deserving of rest and care."

"I honor my needs and celebrate my worth."

Spirit Rituals:

Ancestral Connection: Light a candle or place a small offering on an altar to honor your ancestors. Reflect on the strength they passed down to you.

Meditative Prayer: Spend a few minutes in silent prayer or meditation, focusing on gratitude and guidance.

Creating Your Personal Self-Care Plan

To integrate sacred self-care into your life, create a plan that aligns with your needs and values:

- *Identify Your Priorities:*

What areas of your life feel unbalanced? What practices bring you joy and peace?

....

....

....

....

- *Schedule Time for Yourself:*

Treat self-care as a non-negotiable appointment. Even 10–15 minutes a day can make a difference.

....

....

- *Start Small:*

Begin with one or two self-care practices and gradually build from there.

....

....

....

- *Be Flexible:*

Self-care isn't about perfection. Some days will be busier than others. Focus on what you can do rather than what you can't.

Embracing Self-Care as a Sacred Act

Sacred self-care is a way to remind yourself that you are worthy of love, attention, and care. By honoring your body, mind, and spirit, you create space for healing, joy, and connection with your true self.

In the next chapter, we'll explore how reconnecting with ancestral wisdom can deepen your healing journey and celebrate the strength of those who came before you.

Chapter 10: Reconnecting with Ancestral Wisdom

Ancestral wisdom is a profound source of grounding,

healing, and identity.

For Black women, reconnecting with the strength, resilience, and traditions of our ancestors is not only a way to honor their legacy but also to find empowerment and guidance in our present lives. Ancestral rituals and Afro-diasporic traditions offer tools to heal generational wounds, deepen your connection to your roots, and celebrate your cultural identity.

This chapter explores how to access and embrace ancestral wisdom through meaningful practices, rituals, and traditions that reconnect you to your heritage and spirit.

Why Ancestral Wisdom Matters

Reconnecting with ancestral wisdom serves as a bridge between the past and present, helping you to:

- **Honor Your Lineage:**

Recognize the strength and sacrifices of those who came before you, creating a foundation for your life today.

- **Heal Generational Wounds:**

Many ancestral traditions hold rituals specifically designed to release pain, grief, and trauma carried across generations.

- **Strengthen Your Identity:**

Knowing where you come from helps you embrace who you are and provides a deeper sense of belonging.

- **Draw on Ancestral Strength:**

Your ancestors faced challenges and overcame them. Their resilience is a reminder that their strength flows through you.

Exploring Afro-Diasporic Traditions for Healing

Afro-diasporic traditions are rich with practices that honor ancestors, promote healing, and foster spiritual connection. While specific practices may vary across regions and cultures, here are some commonly shared themes:

- **Altar Building:**

Create a sacred space in your home to honor your ancestors.

Include meaningful items such as photos, candles, flowers, or objects that represent your heritage.

LIBATION RITUALS

HONORING AND INVITING ANCESTRAL GUIDANCE

Libation rituals are ancient practices rooted in many African and Afro-diasporic traditions, serving as a way to honor ancestors, express gratitude, and invite their presence and wisdom into your life. This sacred act is both simple and profound, connecting you to those who came before you and creating a bridge between the spiritual and physical realms.

In this section, you'll learn the significance of libation rituals, how to perform them with intention, and how to incorporate them into your healing journey.

The Significance of Libation Rituals

Libation rituals are deeply symbolic, representing a physical act of offering to ancestors or spiritual forces. When you pour a liquid onto the ground or into a vessel, it symbolizes:

Connection: Acknowledging your link to your ancestors and recognizing the legacy they've passed down.

Gratitude: Thanking your ancestors for their sacrifices, resilience, and the foundation they created for you.

Invitation: Welcoming their guidance, protection, and wisdom as you navigate your journey.

Across cultures, water is seen as a sacred conduit that carries energy and messages. By using water, tea, or wine in a libation ritual, you symbolically nourish your ancestors and affirm their continuing presence in your life.

When to Perform a Libation Ritual

Libation rituals can be performed during:

- *Ancestral Healing Practices:* As part of meditation or other rituals to honor your lineage.
- *Life Transitions:* Before significant events or decisions, such as starting a new job, moving, or embarking on a new chapter.
- *Moments of Gratitude:* Simply to thank your ancestors for their ongoing presence and support.
- *Healing Ceremonies*: To release pain, break cycles, or seek guidance in addressing generational trauma.

How to Perform a Libation Ritual

Here is a step-by-step guide to creating a meaningful libation ritual:

1. **Choose a Sacred Space**
- Select a quiet location where you feel comfortable and connected. This could be outdoors in nature, in a private corner of your home, or near an altar dedicated to your ancestors.
- If you're outdoors, pouring the libation directly onto the earth adds a powerful grounding element. Indoors, you can use a bowl or vessel to hold the liquid.

2. Gather Your Materials

You'll need:

- **A liquid:** Water is the most common choice, symbolizing purity and life, but you can also use tea, wine, or another meaningful beverage.
- **Optional items:** You may include candles, incense, flowers, or photos of your ancestors to enhance the sacredness of the ritual.

3. Set an Intention

Take a moment to reflect on why you're performing the ritual.

- Are you honoring your ancestors?
- Seeking guidance for a specific issue?
- Expressing gratitude for their presence?

State your intention silently or aloud before beginning.

4. Call Upon Your Ancestors

- Stand or kneel in your sacred space, holding the liquid you've chosen.
- Speak the names of your ancestors aloud. If you don't know their names, you can say: "I call upon the ancestors known and unknown, those who love me and guide me."
- Feel their presence surrounding you, offering love and support.

5. Offer the Libation

- Slowly pour the liquid onto the ground, into a vessel, or over a designated area.

As you pour, speak words of gratitude and acknowledgment. For example:

"To the ancestors who endured so I could thrive, I honor your strength."

"To those who came before me, I thank you for your sacrifices and wisdom."

"I invite your guidance and protection as I walk my path of healing."

If you have specific requests, such as strength, clarity, or courage, voice them during this time.

6. Conclude with Gratitude

- After the libation, take a moment of silence to feel the connection you've established.
- Thank your ancestors for their presence, saying: "I am grateful for your love and wisdom. I carry your strength with me."

Incorporating Libation Rituals into Your Life

Libation rituals can become a regular part of your spiritual practice, offering moments of reflection and connection. Here are some ways to make them a consistent part of your routine:

- *Daily Practice:* Begin or end your day with a short libation ritual to honor your ancestors and ground yourself.
- *Special Occasions*: Perform the ritual during family gatherings, birthdays, or anniversaries to celebrate your lineage.
- *Seasonal Ceremonies:* Incorporate libations into seasonal or cultural celebrations, such as harvest festivals or spiritual observances.

Adapting the Ritual to Your Beliefs

Your libation ritual should reflect your personal and cultural values. Feel free to adapt the practice in ways that feel meaningful to you. For example:

- Include prayers, songs, or chants that resonate with your spiritual tradition.
- Use symbolic liquids, such as herbal tea for healing or wine for celebration.
- Add gestures or movements, like bowing or clapping, that signify reverence in your culture.

Final Reflections

A libation ritual is more than an act of pouring liquid—it's a profound gesture of connection, gratitude, and empowerment. By acknowledging your ancestors in this sacred way, you honor their legacy and invite their wisdom into your life.

Each time you perform a libation ritual, you reaffirm the strength of your lineage and your commitment to healing and growth. Whether practiced alone or shared with family, this ritual is a powerful reminder that you are never walking your path alone—your ancestors are with you, guiding and supporting you every step of the way.

- **Drumming and Music:**

Many Afro-diasporic cultures use rhythm and song as a way to connect with the divine and honor ancestors.

Play or listen to traditional music to ground yourself and celebrate your roots.

- **Herbal Practices:**

Explore the use of herbs like sage, rosemary, or African basil for cleansing, protection, and spiritual healing.

Create teas, baths, or incense to incorporate these traditions into your self-care routine.

Ancestral Rituals to Reconnect and Heal

Invocation of Ancestors:

- Sit in a quiet space, light a candle, and call upon your ancestors.
- Speak their names if you know them, or simply say: "*I honor the ancestors who guide me, known and unknown.*"
- Reflect on their strength and invite their wisdom into your life.

Letter to Your Ancestors:

- Write a letter to your ancestors, sharing your gratitude, struggles, or questions.

....

....

....

....

....

....

- Place the letter on your altar or burn it as an offering, symbolizing your connection to them.

Meditation with Ancestral Imagery:

- Close your eyes and visualize a gathering of your ancestors surrounding you.
- Imagine them offering you their love, protection, and encouragement as you move forward in your journey.

Healing through Storytelling:

- Share stories about your family or learn more about your heritage through conversations with elders.
- If information about your family history is limited, explore cultural traditions tied to your ancestry.

Learning from the Past to Empower the Present

Your ancestors' lives were filled with lessons, both from their triumphs and their hardships. Reflect on these questions to integrate their wisdom into your own life:

What challenges did my ancestors face, and how did they overcome them?

....

....

....

....

What strengths or values have been passed down to me through my lineage?

....

....

....

How can I honor their legacy while forging my own path?

....

....

....

....

Exercises to Deepen Connection

- **Ancestor Gratitude Journal:**
  - ✓ Write daily or weekly reflections on the ways your ancestors have influenced your life.
  - ✓ Include moments when you felt their presence or guidance.
- **Cultural Exploration:**
  - ✓ Research traditions, foods, dances, or spiritual practices tied to your ancestry.
  - ✓ Try incorporating one new practice into your life each month.
- **Ritual for Releasing Generational Pain:**
  - ✓ Light a white candle and hold an object that represents your lineage.
  - ✓ Speak aloud the pain you wish to release, such as: "I release the fear, anger, and grief passed down through my lineage. I honor my ancestors and choose healing."
- **Creative Expression:**
  - ✓ Create art, music, or poetry inspired by your heritage as a way to celebrate your connection to your roots.

Embracing Your Ancestral Power

Reconnecting with your ancestors is not just about looking back—it's about drawing on their strength to create a better present and future. By embracing their wisdom, you honor the resilience and courage they passed down to you while paving the way for your own unique path.

In the next chapter, we will explore how to celebrate your personal growth and healing through rituals of self-recognition and empowerment.

Chapter 11: Rituals of Celebration: Honoring Your Growth

Healing is a journey, not a destination.

Along the way, it's easy to focus on what's left to accomplish while overlooking how far you've already come. Celebrating your progress is not only an act of gratitude for your efforts but also a way to reinforce the positive changes you've made.

This chapter is about creating personal rituals to honor your growth, acknowledge your achievements, and infuse joy and pride into your healing journey. By celebrating yourself, you recognize your strength, resilience, and commitment to becoming your true self.

Why Celebration Matters

Acknowledging your growth is a vital part of healing. Here's why celebration should be an integral part of your journey:

✓ **It Reinforces Positive Change:**

Celebrating your wins, big or small, strengthens the habits and behaviors that support your growth.

✓ **It Builds Self-Confidence:**

Recognizing your achievements reminds you of your capabilities and empowers you to keep moving forward.

✓ **It Shifts Your Focus:**

Instead of dwelling on what's left to do, celebration centers your attention on your progress and resilience.

✓ **It Invites Joy:**

Healing can feel heavy at times. Celebrating adds lightness and reminds you that joy is a crucial part of the process.

Creating Rituals to Honor Your Growth

Celebration doesn't have to be elaborate—it's about intentionality and meaning. Here are ways to create rituals that reflect and honor your journey:

- **Personal Reflection Rituals:**

Gratitude Journaling: At the end of each week or month, write down moments when you felt proud, strong, or accomplished.

Milestone Journals: Create a journal specifically for marking key moments in your healing journey, such as overcoming a fear, setting a boundary, or forgiving someone.

- **Symbolic Acts:**

Lighting a Candle: Light a candle and take a few moments to reflect on your progress. Speak affirmations like: "I honor the work I have done and the person I am becoming."

Releasing Rituals: Write down old fears or limiting beliefs you've let go of, and burn or shred the paper as a symbolic act of release.

- **Physical Celebrations:**

Dance It Out: Create a playlist of songs that make you feel strong and joyful, and dance as a way of celebrating your growth.

Self-Care Treats: Gift yourself something meaningful, whether it's a special meal, a new book, or time alone to recharge.

- **Creative Expression:**

Use art, poetry, or journaling to create something that represents your journey. This could be a vision board, a poem about your growth, or a painting inspired by your experiences.

Marking Milestones in Your Journey

Sometimes, you may want to celebrate a specific milestone in a bigger way. Here are examples of milestones and ways to honor them:

- **Setting Boundaries: Prioritizing Your Needs and Celebrating Your Growth**

Setting boundaries is a powerful act of self-love and self-respect. It's about defining what is and isn't acceptable in your relationships, work, and personal life. Boundaries protect your energy, time, and emotional well-being, creating space for you to thrive.

Yet, setting boundaries isn't always easy. For many, especially Black women, societal pressures to constantly give, support, and "be strong" can make the act of saying no feel uncomfortable or even guilt-inducing. But setting boundaries is not selfish—it's necessary. It's a way to reclaim control over your life and honor your worth.

Once you've taken the brave step of establishing a boundary, it's equally important to celebrate your progress and reinforce your commitment to yourself. A self-care day is the perfect way to acknowledge the boundary you've set, recharge your energy, and reflect on the empowerment that comes with honoring your needs.

Why Setting Boundaries Matters

Protecting Your Energy:

- Boundaries help you conserve your emotional and physical energy, ensuring you have enough to focus on what truly matters.

Reducing Stress:

- Saying no to draining situations or relationships prevents burnout and allows you to approach life with balance and calm.

Fostering Healthier Relationships:

- Clear boundaries create mutual respect and understanding in relationships, allowing them to flourish.

Reinforcing Your Worth:

- Each time you set and uphold a boundary, you affirm that your time, feelings, and well-being are valuable.

Celebrating the Boundaries You Set

After setting a boundary, it's important to take time to celebrate your progress. This not only reinforces the boundary itself but also strengthens your self-esteem and commitment to self-care.

Here's how to celebrate and honor yourself after setting a boundary:

1. Plan a Self-Care Day

A self-care day is an opportunity to focus entirely on your well-being and recharge your mind, body, and spirit.

How to Create Your Self-Care Day

Set the Tone:

- Begin the day with intention. Reflect on the boundary you've set and acknowledge the courage it took to establish it.
- Light a candle, meditate, or journal about how this boundary has positively impacted your life.

Choose Activities That Nourish You:

- *Relaxation*: Take a long bath, listen to calming music, or spend time in nature.
- *Creativity*: Engage in activities like painting, writing, or cooking that bring you joy and allow for self-expression.
- *Movement*: Practice yoga, dance, or take a walk to reconnect with your body.
- *Connection*: Spend time with supportive friends or loved ones who respect and uplift you.

Treat Yourself:

Reward yourself with something special, such as your favorite meal, a new book, or a small gift that reminds you of your worth.

Unplug:

Disconnect from work, social media, or anything that drains your energy. Use this time to focus solely on yourself.

2. Reflect on Your Growth

Take time during your self-care day to reflect on how setting boundaries has impacted your life.

Journaling Prompts

What was the boundary I set, and why was it important to me?

....

....

....

How has this boundary improved my emotional or physical well-being?

....

....

....

What challenges did I face in setting this boundary, and how did I overcome them?

....

....

....

How can I continue to honor this boundary moving forward?

....

....

....

By documenting your reflections, you create a tangible record of your growth and a reminder of your strength.

3. Reaffirm Your Commitment to Self-Care

Boundaries are an ongoing practice. Use your self-care day to reaffirm your commitment to prioritizing your needs and maintaining the boundaries you've set.

Affirmations to Support Your Boundaries

"I have the right to prioritize my well-being without guilt."

"Setting boundaries is a form of self-respect and self-love."

"My time and energy are valuable, and I choose to spend them wisely."

"I release any guilt or fear associated with saying no."

Repeat these affirmations throughout the day to strengthen your resolve and empower yourself.

4. Visualize the Life You're Building

Boundaries are not just about what you're saying no to—they're about creating space for what you want to say yes to.

Visualization Exercise

- Close your eyes and imagine a version of your life where your boundaries are consistently respected.
- Picture yourself thriving in healthy relationships, pursuing your passions, and feeling balanced and fulfilled.
- Focus on how this version of your life makes you feel—joyful, empowered, and at peace.

Visualization helps you stay motivated to uphold your boundaries, reminding you of the positive outcomes they create.

Tips for Maintaining Your Boundaries

Communicate Clearly:

When setting a boundary, be direct and specific about your needs. For example: "I need time to myself after work, so I won't be available for calls during that time."

Anticipate Pushback:

Some people may challenge your boundaries, especially if they've benefited from you not having them. Stay firm and remind yourself why the boundary is important.

Practice Saying No:

If saying no feels uncomfortable, start small. Practice declining minor requests and work your way up to more significant situations.

Seek Support:

Surround yourself with people who respect your boundaries and encourage your growth.

Regularly Reevaluate:

Your needs may change over time. Periodically assess your boundaries to ensure they still align with your goals and values.

The Transformative Power of Boundaries

Setting boundaries isn't just an act of protection—it's a declaration of self-worth. By honoring your needs, you create space for joy, balance, and growth in your life. Celebrating your boundaries with a self-care day reinforces this commitment, reminding you that prioritizing yourself is not only okay—it's essential.

Each boundary you set is a step toward a more authentic and fulfilling life. Embrace the power of saying no to what doesn't serve you, so you can say yes to the things that truly matter.

Letting Go of Resentment:

Host a personal release ceremony with candles, incense, or music that resonates with freedom and peace.

Forgiving Yourself or Others:

Write a letter to yourself or the person you forgave, expressing gratitude for the strength it took to forgive.

Reconnecting with Joy:

Plan a day to do something you love—visit a park, try a new hobby, or spend time with loved ones.

Daily Practices to Celebrate Yourself

You don't have to wait for a major milestone to honor your journey. Here are small, daily ways to celebrate yourself:

Morning Affirmations: Start your day with affirmations like:

"I celebrate my growth every day."

"I honor my journey, no matter how small the steps."

Mirror Celebrations: Look at yourself in the mirror and say one thing you're proud of from the day before.

Joy Breaks: Take a few minutes each day to do something that brings you joy, like listening to a favorite song or sipping tea in quiet reflection.

Nightly Wins: Before bed, reflect on one thing you did well that day, no matter how small.

Exercises to Acknowledge Your Achievements

Acknowledging your achievements is an essential part of the healing process. It allows you to reflect on your growth, celebrate your strengths, and stay motivated for the journey ahead. Recognizing how far you've come isn't about perfection; it's about honoring the steps you've taken, the lessons you've learned, and the resilience you've built along the way.

In this section, you'll find detailed exercises to help you reflect on your progress, connect with your strengths, and visualize the empowered version of yourself that you're becoming. These exercises are designed to deepen your self-awareness and remind you that every step forward—no matter how small—is worth celebrating.

1. The Growth Timeline

Creating a timeline of your healing journey is a powerful way to visualize your progress and recognize the key moments that have shaped your growth.

How to Create Your Growth Timeline

✓ **Gather Your Tools:**

Use a journal, a large sheet of paper, or digital tools like a word processor or drawing app.

✓ **Identify Milestones:**

Reflect on the significant moments in your healing journey.

These could include:

Times when you confronted a fear or challenge.

....

....

....

Breakthroughs in understanding your emotions or patterns.

....

....

....

Moments of forgiveness, whether toward yourself or others.

....

....

....

Decisions to set boundaries or prioritize self-care.

....

....

....

Example Milestones: "January: I set my first boundary with a family member." or "March: I forgave myself for a past mistake."

✓ **Map It Out:**

Draw a line to represent your journey and mark each milestone along the way.

Next to each milestone, write a brief description of what happened and why it was significant.

✓ **Reflect on Your Timeline:**

Spend time looking at your timeline and ask yourself:

What have I learned from these moments?

....

....

How have these milestones shaped the person I am today?

....

....

Taking It Further

- *Add Visual Elements:* Include symbols, colors, or drawings that represent each milestone.
- *Write a Letter:* Compose a letter to your past self, thanking them for their courage and reflecting on how far you've come.

....

....

....

....

....

....

....

2. Celebrate Your Strengths

Your healing journey has likely revealed qualities you may not have recognized before. This exercise helps you identify and honor those strengths, fostering self-confidence and appreciation.

- **How to Celebrate Your Strengths**

Reflect on Your Journey:

Think about the challenges you've faced and the qualities you've drawn upon to navigate them.

....

....

....

Make a List of Strengths:

Write down the qualities you've developed or discovered during your journey.

Examples include:

Resilience: "I've bounced back from setbacks with determination."

Courage: "I've faced fears and taken steps toward healing."

Compassion: "I've learned to be kinder to myself and others."

....

....

....

Acknowledge Each Strength:

For each quality, write a sentence or two about how it has helped you. For example:

"My resilience has allowed me to keep going even when things felt impossible."

"My courage has empowered me to confront painful truths and take control of my life."

....

....

....

....

....

....

....

....

....

....

....

....

....

....

- **Taking It Further**

Create a Strength Collage: Gather images, words, or symbols that represent your strengths and arrange them into a visual collage.

Share Your Strengths: Talk about your strengths with a trusted friend or loved one. Hearing their perspective can deepen your appreciation of yourself.

3. **Visualize Your Future Self**

Visualization is a powerful tool that helps you connect with the person you're becoming. By imagining your future self looking back on your journey, you can gain clarity, inspiration, and a sense of purpose.

- **How to Visualize Your Future Self**

Find a Quiet Space:

Sit comfortably in a quiet place where you won't be disturbed. Close your eyes and take a few deep breaths to center yourself.

Picture Your Future Self:

Imagine yourself 5 or 10 years into the future. Visualize the person you've become after continuing your healing journey.

Notice the details:

- o   What do you look like?
- o   How do you carry yourself?
- o   What emotions do you radiate? (e.g., peace, confidence, joy)

Reflect on Your Journey:

Picture your future self, looking back on the milestones you've achieved. Imagine her saying:

"Thank you for having the courage to start this journey."

"Every step you took brought me to where I am today."

Invite Guidance:

Ask your future self:

What advice do you have for me right now?

....

....

....

....

....

....

What should I focus on to continue growing and healing?

....

....

....

....

....

Listen for the answers that come to you intuitively.

- **Taking It Further**

Write a Letter from Your Future Self: Imagine your future self writing to you in the present. What would she say to encourage, support, or inspire you?

....

....

....

....

....

....

....

Create a Vision Board: Include images, words, and symbols that represent your future self and the life you're working toward.

- **Bringing It All Together**

Reflecting on your achievements is not just about celebrating the past—it's about affirming your ability to continue growing, healing, and evolving. By creating a timeline, recognizing your strengths, and visualizing your future self, you build a deeper sense of connection to your journey and your potential.

Remember, every step you take—no matter how small— matters. You are proof of your own resilience, and your story is a testament to the power of growth and transformation. Keep acknowledging and celebrating your progress, because you are becoming exactly the person you are meant to be.

Final Thoughts

Honoring your growth isn't just about the destination—it's about celebrating every step you take along the way. Rituals of celebration remind you that healing is an ongoing process, and every moment of progress is worth acknowledging.

In the final chapter, we'll explore how to sustain your healing and growth while building a legacy of light and empowerment for the generations to come.

Chapter 12: Writing Your New Story: Redefining Your Identity

Every experience you've lived has contributed to the story you tell about yourself—but that story is not set in stone.

Through intentional reflection and conscious effort, you can rewrite your narrative, shedding limiting beliefs and embracing a version of yourself rooted in empowerment and authenticity.

This chapter is about reclaiming the pen to write your own story. With journaling prompts and practical tools, you'll explore how to let go of old narratives that no longer serve you and craft a life aligned with your truth and values.

Why Redefining Your Identity Matters

The stories we tell ourselves shape how we see the world and our place in it. Often, these stories are influenced by:

Childhood experiences: Beliefs about your worth, capabilities, or potential often stem from what you were told or how you were treated growing up.

Societal expectations: Messages about race, gender, and culture can reinforce limiting beliefs about who you "should" be.

Past traumas: Painful experiences can leave you feeling stuck, defining yourself by the wounds instead of the healing.

By rewriting your story, you reclaim the power to define yourself on your own terms.

<u>The Process of Rewriting Your Story</u>

- **Identify Old Narratives:**

Reflect on the beliefs or stories you've internalized that no longer serve you.

For example:

"I always have to be strong."

"I'm not good enough to succeed."

"My voice doesn't matter."

- **Challenge Limiting Beliefs:**

Question the validity of these stories. Ask yourself:

Is this really true?

Where did this belief come from?

What evidence do I have that contradicts this story?

- **Define Who You Want to Be:**

Envision the person you want to become. What qualities, beliefs, and values define this version of you?

- **Rewrite the Narrative:**

Replace old, limiting beliefs with empowering ones.

- ✓ Instead of: "I always have to be strong," say: "I am strong, but I can also ask for help when I need it."
- ✓ Instead of: "I'm not good enough to succeed," say: "I am capable, and my efforts bring me closer to success."

- **Journaling Prompts to Rewrite Your Story**

Use these prompts to explore and redefine your identity:

Reflecting on the Past:

What is a story I've told myself about who I am?

....

....

Where did this story come from, and how has it shaped my life?

....

....

Challenging Limiting Beliefs:

What beliefs about myself are holding me back?

....

....

....

What would I say to a friend who believed the same thing about themselves?

....

....

....

Envisioning the Future:

Who do I want to be in one year, five years, or ten years?

....

....

....

What steps can I take today to align myself with that vision?

....

....

....

Celebrating Strengths:

What strengths or qualities have helped me overcome challenges?

....

....

....

How can I use these strengths to support my growth?

....

....

....

Crafting Affirmations:

Write three affirmations that reflect the person you are becoming. For example:

"I am worthy of love and respect."

"I have the power to create the life I want."

"My voice is valuable and deserves to be heard."

....

....

....

- **Tools for Creating an Empowering Narrative**

Vision Board:

Create a visual representation of the life you want to build. Include images, words, and symbols that reflect your dreams, values, and goals.

....

....

....

Daily Affirmations:

Write affirmations that resonate with your new story and repeat them daily to reinforce your beliefs.

....

....

....

....

Future Self Letter:

Write a letter from your future self to your present self, describing the life you've built and the obstacles you've overcome.

....

....

....

....

....

The "I Am" Exercise:

Complete the sentence "I am..." with positive and empowering descriptors.

Example: "I am resilient. I am compassionate. I am enough."

....

....

....

....

....

- **Living Your New Story**

Rewriting your story is an ongoing process. It's not about erasing the past but about choosing how you want it to influence your future. Every time you challenge a limiting belief, set a boundary, or take a step toward your dreams, you are adding to the story of your empowerment and authenticity.

In your new story:

YOU ARE NOT DEFINED BY WHAT HAS HAPPENED TO YOU BUT BY HOW YOU HAVE CHOSEN TO GROW.

YOU HAVE THE POWER TO ALIGN YOUR LIFE WITH YOUR DEEPEST VALUES AND DESIRES.

YOU ARE THE AUTHOR OF YOUR NARRATIVE, AND YOUR POSSIBILITIES ARE LIMITLESS.

Final Thoughts

Your story is yours to write. By shedding the narratives that no longer serve you and embracing the truth of who you are, you create space for a life filled with authenticity, joy, and purpose.

In the next chapter, we'll explore how to sustain your healing journey and turn your growth into a legacy that inspires others.

Part 4: Integration and Continuation

Chapter 13: From Pain to Power: Living as Your Authentic Self

Healing is a journey, not a destination.

The lessons you've learned and the growth you've achieved are meant to be integrated into your daily life, transforming pain into power and allowing you to live as your most authentic self. This chapter focuses on practical strategies for incorporating what you've learned into your routines, maintaining balance, and continuing your Shadow Work journey with intention and purpose.

The Transition from Healing to Thriving

As you reflect on your journey, it's important to recognize that healing is not about erasing pain—it's about transforming it. Moving from pain to power means:

- **Acknowledging Your Growth:** Celebrate how far you've come and recognize the strength you've developed.
- **Living Authentically:** Align your actions, decisions, and relationships with your true self.
- **Embracing Imperfection:** Understand that healing is ongoing and doesn't require perfection.

- **Integrating What You've Learned**

Daily Mindfulness Practices: Cultivating Presence and Balance

Mindfulness is the practice of being fully present in the moment without judgment. It allows you to focus on what's happening here and now, rather than getting caught up in the past or worrying about the future. Incorporating mindfulness into your daily routine can reduce stress, improve emotional regulation, and foster a deeper connection with yourself.

Starting your day with mindfulness is especially powerful. It sets a positive tone, grounding you before the demands of the day take hold. Whether you have 5 minutes or an hour, mindfulness practices can help you center your thoughts, nurture your well-being, and approach your day with clarity and intention.

Why Daily Mindfulness Matters

- o **Reduces Stress**: Mindfulness helps you step out of the cycle of overthinking and approach challenges with calm and focus.
- o **Improves Emotional Resilience**: Regular mindfulness enhances your ability to respond to emotions thoughtfully rather than react impulsively.
- o **Promotes Self-Awareness:** By being present, you develop a deeper understanding of your thoughts, emotions, and needs.
- o **Enhances Focus:** Mindfulness trains your brain to concentrate on what matters most, improving productivity and decision-making.

How to Incorporate Mindfulness into Your Morning Routine

Here are a few simple yet impactful ways to practice mindfulness daily:

1. Mindful Breathing

Breathing is one of the most accessible tools for mindfulness. By focusing on your breath, you can calm your mind and reconnect with your body.

How to Practice

- Find a quiet place to sit or stand comfortably.
- Close your eyes or lower your gaze to minimize distractions.
- Take a slow, deep breath in through your nose, counting to four. Hold for a count of four, then exhale through your mouth for a count of six.
- Repeat this cycle for 5–10 breaths, focusing on the sensation of the air entering and leaving your body.
- If your mind wanders, gently bring your attention back to your breath.

Benefits

- Reduces anxiety and stress.
- Grounds you in the present moment.
- Provides a quick reset anytime during the day.

2. Morning Meditation

Meditation is a deeper mindfulness practice that allows you to cultivate inner peace and clarity.

How to Practice

- o Set aside 5–15 minutes in the morning. Sit in a quiet, comfortable spot.
- o Close your eyes and focus on your breath, a mantra, or a visualization.
- o When thoughts arise (and they will), acknowledge them without judgment and gently return to your point of focus.
- o End the session by setting an intention for the day, such as:
- ✓ "Today, I will approach challenges with patience."
- ✓ "I will focus on progress, not perfection."

Benefits

- o Helps you start the day with a calm and focused mindset.
- o Encourages self-awareness and emotional balance.
- o Supports long-term mental health and resilience.

3. Gratitude Journaling

Journaling in the morning is a great way to focus your mind and set a positive tone for the day. Gratitude journaling, in particular, shifts your perspective to abundance and appreciation.

How to Practice

- o Keep a notebook and pen by your bed or in your morning space.
- o Write down three things you're grateful for each morning. These can be big or small, such as:
  - ✓ "I'm grateful for a good night's sleep."
  - ✓ "I'm grateful for the support of my friends."
  - ✓ "I'm grateful for the opportunity to start fresh today."
- o Reflect on why these things matter to you and how they make you feel.

Benefits

- o Promotes positivity and reduces stress.
- o Encourages mindfulness by focusing on the present moment.
- o Builds resilience by reinforcing a sense of abundance and gratitude.

4. Body Scan Practice

A body scan is a mindfulness technique that helps you reconnect with your physical self and release tension.

How to Practice

- Lie down or sit comfortably in a quiet space. Close your eyes.
- Begin at the top of your head and slowly bring your attention to each part of your body, moving downward.
- Notice any tension, discomfort, or sensations.
- With each exhale, imagine releasing any tightness or stress in that area.
- Continue until you've scanned your entire body, from head to toe.

Benefits

- Promotes relaxation and body awareness.
- Helps release physical tension and stress.
- Encourages a sense of grounding and presence.

5. Mindful Intention-Setting

Setting an intention for the day is a mindful way to align your actions with your values and goals.

How to Practice

- o Take a moment to reflect on what you want to focus on or accomplish during the day.
- o Phrase your intention as a positive affirmation, such as:
    - ✓ "I will prioritize my well-being today."
    - ✓ "I will approach my work with creativity and focus."
- o Write your intention in a journal or repeat it silently to yourself throughout the day.

Benefits

- o Provides clarity and direction for your day.
- o Encourages mindfulness by focusing on what truly matters.
- o Helps you stay grounded during challenging moments.

Creating a Consistent Practice

Mindfulness is most effective when practiced regularly. Here are some tips to make daily mindfulness a habit:

> ➤ **Start Small:** Begin with just 5 minutes each morning and gradually increase the time as it feels comfortable.
> ➤ **Set a Reminder:** Use an alarm or note to remind yourself to practice mindfulness each morning.
> ➤ **Make It Enjoyable:** Incorporate elements you enjoy, such as soothing music, candles, or a favorite journal.
> ➤ **Be Flexible:** Life happens, and it's okay to adjust your routine as needed. Even a single mindful breath can make a difference.

Final Thoughts

Daily mindfulness practices are small but powerful steps toward a more balanced and intentional life. By grounding yourself in the morning, you create a foundation of calm and clarity that carries you through the day.

Remember, mindfulness is not about doing it perfectly—it's about showing up for yourself, moment by moment, with kindness and curiosity. Whether you meditate, journal, or simply take a few deep breaths, each practice is a gift you give to yourself.

Make mindfulness your daily ritual, and watch as it transforms not just your mornings but your entire way of being.

Journaling as a Lifelong Tool

Continue journaling as a way to check in with yourself, reflect on your emotions, and track your growth. Questions to explore include:

What did I learn about myself today?

....

....

How can I honor my needs tomorrow?

....

....

Embracing Vulnerability:

Practice showing up authentically in your relationships. Share your thoughts and feelings openly with those you trust.

Setting Intentional Goals:

Use what you've learned to set goals that align with your values and desires. For example:

> ➤ Strengthen relationships that uplift you.
> ➤ Dedicate time to passions or hobbies that bring you joy.

Strategies for Maintaining Balance

Establish Healthy Boundaries:

Protect your time and energy by saying no to things that don't serve your well-being.

Regularly assess your commitments to ensure they align with your priorities.

Prioritize Self-Care:

Make self-care non-negotiable. Incorporate daily rituals, such as a gratitude practice or time for relaxation, to maintain balance.

Surround Yourself with Support:

Build a community of people who understand and support your growth. This could include friends, mentors, or online groups focused on healing and empowerment.

Revisit Shadow Work:

Shadow Work is not a one-time process. Periodically revisit your triggers and explore new layers of growth. Use tools like journaling, therapy, or meditation to dive deeper when needed.

Tips for Continuing Your Shadow Work Journey

Be Patient with Yourself:

Growth is not linear. There will be moments when old wounds resurface or progress feels slow. Treat yourself with compassion and kindness.

Create Rituals for Reflection:

Set aside time each month to reflect on your journey. Ask yourself:

What have I learned about myself recently?

....

....

What challenges have I faced, and how did I handle them?

....

....

Celebrate Milestones:

Acknowledge your progress by celebrating your wins, both big and small. This could be as simple as treating yourself to something special or writing a gratitude letter to yourself.

Stay Curious:

Healing is an ongoing exploration. Stay open to discovering new layers of yourself and embracing the lessons they bring.

Living as Your Authentic Self

Authenticity means embracing all parts of who you are—your strengths, your vulnerabilities, your past, and your future. To live authentically:

Trust Your Intuition:

Listen to your inner voice when making decisions. Trust that you know what's best for you.

Honor Your Truth:

Speak and act in ways that align with your values, even when it feels challenging.

Show Up Fully:

Let go of the need to be perfect. Living authentically means showing up as your whole self, flaws and all.

Exercises to Reinforce Your Growth

Crafting a Personal Mission Statement

Creating a personal mission statement is a powerful exercise that helps you define your values, clarify your goals, and stay focused on the person you are becoming. It serves as a guiding light, reminding you of what matters most and inspiring you to align your actions with your aspirations.

This section walks you through the process of crafting a meaningful mission statement and explores how it can reinforce your growth and empowerment.

What Is a Personal Mission Statement?

A personal mission statement is a declaration of who you are, what you value, and what you're striving to achieve in your life. It's more than just a set of goals—it's a reflection of your core beliefs and the legacy you want to create.

Why Create One?

> *Clarity:* Helps you define your priorities and focus your energy.
> *Motivation:* Acts as a reminder of your purpose, especially during challenging times.

> ➢ ***Alignment:*** Ensures that your daily actions are consistent with your long-term vision.
> ➢ ***Empowerment***: Reinforces your commitment to growth and self-care.

Steps to Create Your Personal Mission Statement

1. Reflect on Your Values

Your mission statement should be rooted in your values—the principles that guide your decisions and define what's meaningful to you.

<u>Exercise</u>

Write down a list of values that resonate with you. Examples include:

- Authenticity
- Resilience
- Growth
- Compassion
- Creativity
- Balance

Circle the 3–5 values that feel most important to you right now.

Write them here:

....

....

....

....

2. Identify Your Goals

Think about the areas of your life where you want to grow or create change. These could include personal development, relationships, career, health, or community.

<u>Exercise</u>

Write down your goals for the next year, five years, or even a lifetime.

Ask yourself:

What do I want to achieve?

....

....

....

....

What kind of person do I want to become?

....

....

....

What legacy do I want to leave behind?

....

....

....

3. Envision Your Best Self

Take a moment to imagine the most empowered, authentic version of yourself. What qualities does this version of you embody? How do they interact with the world?

<u>Exercise</u>

Close your eyes and visualize your best self.

Answer the following prompts:

"My best self is…"

....

....

....

"My best self prioritizes…"

....

....

....

"My best self shows up as…"

....

....

....

....

4. Write Your Mission Statement

Using your reflections, craft a statement that captures your values, goals, and aspirations.

<u>Example Frameworks</u>

Value-Oriented:

"I am committed to living authentically, prioritizing my well-being, and embracing my growth with compassion and courage."

....

....

....

Goal-Oriented:

"My mission is to create a life of balance and fulfillment by nurturing my relationships, pursuing my passions, and honoring my mental and physical health."

....

....

....

Purpose-Oriented:

"I aim to inspire others by living as a testament to resilience, self-love, and the power of transformation."

....

....

....

Refining Your Mission Statement

Once you've written a draft, take time to refine it.

- *Keep It Concise:* A mission statement should be clear and easy to remember. Aim for 1–3 sentences.
- *Make It Personal:* Use words and phrases that feel authentic to you. Avoid generic language that doesn't resonate with your unique journey.

Test Its Relevance: Ask yourself:

- Does this reflect who I am and who I want to become?
- Does this inspire me to take action?

Incorporating Your Mission Statement into Daily Life

A mission statement is most powerful when it's actively integrated into your life. Here's how to use it as a tool for growth:

1. Display It Prominently

Write your mission statement on a note card or piece of paper and place it somewhere you'll see often, such as your desk, mirror, or phone background.

2. Use It as a Morning Affirmation

Start each day by reading your mission statement aloud. This reinforces your commitment to your values and goals.

3. Check In Regularly

Reflect on your mission statement during weekly or monthly check-ins. Ask yourself:

Am I living in alignment with my mission?

....

What adjustments can I make to stay on track?

....

4. Apply It to Decision-Making

When faced with choices or challenges, use your mission statement as a compass. Ask:

Does this decision align with my mission?

....

Is this action consistent with my values and goals?

....

Examples of Personal Mission Statements

For Growth and Resilience:

"I am dedicated to becoming the strongest, most authentic version of myself by embracing challenges, learning from my experiences, and living with courage and integrity."

....

....

....

For Balance and Self-Care:

"My mission is to prioritize my well-being, create harmony between work and rest, and cultivate relationships that uplift and inspire me."

....

....

....

For Community and Impact:

"I aim to use my voice and talents to uplift others, create positive change, and build a legacy of kindness and empowerment."

....

....

....

Revisiting and Evolving Your Mission Statement

Your mission statement is a living document. As you grow and evolve, your values and goals may shift. Periodically revisit your statement to ensure it reflects your current priorities and aspirations.

Check-In Prompts

Does my mission statement still resonate with me?

....

....

What changes have occurred in my life since I wrote it?

....

....

....

....

How can I refine my mission to reflect my growth?

....

....

....

....

....

Final Thoughts

Creating a personal mission statement is an act of self-empowerment. It helps you define your purpose, align with your values, and stay focused on the life you want to create. By revisiting and living by your mission statement, you reinforce your commitment to growth and authenticity every day.

Your mission statement is more than just words—it's a reflection of your journey and a declaration of your future. Write it with intention, revisit it with pride, and live it with purpose.

Reflective Journaling

At the end of each week, reflect on:

What moments felt most authentic to me?

....

....

What challenges did I face, and how did I grow from them?

....

....

Gratitude Practice:

Write down three things you're grateful for each day to shift your focus toward positivity and abundance.

....

....

....

Vision Board for the Future:

Create a vision board that represents the life you want to build and revisit it regularly to stay inspired.

....

....

....

···

···

···

···

···

···

Final Thoughts

Moving from pain to power is a journey of integration, balance, and authenticity. As you continue to grow, remember that healing is a lifelong process. Celebrate your progress, honor your resilience, and trust in your ability to create a life that reflects your true self.

In the final chapter, we'll explore how your healing journey can inspire and uplift others, creating a legacy of light and empowerment for future generations.

Chapter 14: Building a Legacy: Healing for Future Generations

Healing is not just a gift to yourself—it's a powerful act of love and resistance that can ripple through your family, community, and future generations.

By confronting your pain, breaking cycles of trauma, and reclaiming your authentic self, you're creating a legacy of healing and empowerment that transcends your individual journey.

This chapter explores how to share your healing with others, inspire change in those around you, and ensure that the lessons you've learned become a foundation of strength and resilience for generations to come.

- **Why Your Healing Matters for Future Generations**

Breaking the Cycle:

Many of the struggles you've faced may have been inherited from past generations. By healing yourself, you disrupt patterns of pain and create new, healthier pathways for those who follow.

Leading by Example:

When you prioritize healing, authenticity, and self-care, you show others—especially younger generations—that it's possible to live with intention and freedom.

Creating a New Narrative:

By living your truth, you rewrite the story of what it means to be strong, vulnerable, and whole. This inspires others to do the same.

- **Sharing Your Healing Journey**

Your story has the power to heal and uplift others. Here are ways to share your journey meaningfully:

Tell Your Story with Courage:

Share your experiences with trusted family members, friends, or community groups. Be open about the challenges you've faced and the growth you've achieved.

Document Your Journey:

Keep a journal, write a memoir, or record videos about your healing process. These can serve as a guide and inspiration for future generations.

Create Space for Dialogue:

Start conversations about healing, mental health, and personal growth within your family or community. Normalizing these topics can break taboos and encourage others to seek their own paths of healing.

Mentor and Support:

Offer guidance to younger family members, friends, or mentees who may be navigating challenges similar to those you've faced. Share the tools and insights that have helped you.

- **Healing as an Act of Love and Resistance**

For Black women, healing is deeply connected to community and culture. It is an act of resistance against systems that have historically devalued your voice, your worth, and your humanity.

Resisting Oppression Through Self-Care:

Prioritizing your well-being is a radical act in a world that often expects you to neglect yourself for others.

Reclaiming Your Heritage:

Honor and incorporate ancestral wisdom into your life. By embracing the traditions, stories, and resilience of those who came before you, you build a stronger connection to your roots.

Cultivating Community Healing:

Share the tools and practices you've learned with others, fostering a collective journey of healing and empowerment.

Practical Steps to Build a Legacy of Healing

Celebrate Your Family's Strengths:

Focus on the positive qualities and values passed down through your lineage, such as resilience, creativity, or kindness.

Share stories of triumph and strength to inspire pride and connection.

Start New Traditions:

Create rituals that promote healing and connection, such as family journaling sessions, gratitude circles, or annual self-care retreats.

Teach Emotional Awareness:

Help younger generations understand the importance of acknowledging and expressing their emotions.

Introduce them to tools like journaling, meditation, or therapy.

Advocate for Change:

Use your voice to push for systemic changes that support healing and equity in your community, such as mental health resources, education, or mentorship programs.

Create a Legacy of Learning:

Share books, music, art, or cultural traditions that have influenced your journey. Pass these down as a source of inspiration and wisdom.

<u>**Exercises to Strengthen Your Legacy**</u>

Letter to Future Generations:

Write a letter to your children, grandchildren, or other future family members. Share your journey, your lessons, and your hopes for them.

....

....

....

....

....

....

....

....

....

Family Healing Journal:

Start a family journal where each member can contribute reflections, gratitude, or personal stories.

Vision for the Future:

Create a family vision board, highlighting the values, goals, and dreams you want to prioritize as a collective.

....

....

....

....

Final Thoughts

Your healing is a powerful gift that extends far beyond yourself. By breaking cycles, sharing your journey, and creating new traditions, you pave the way for future generations to live with greater freedom, self-awareness, and joy.

The work you do today transforms not only your own life but also the lives of those who come after you. This legacy of healing is a testament to your strength, love, and commitment to creating a better world—for yourself, your family, and your community.

You've reclaimed your power, healed your pain, and embraced your true self. Now, as you move forward, let your journey inspire others to do the same, creating a ripple effect of healing and empowerment that spans generations.

Bonus Chapter: Guided Meditations for Healing and Empowerment

Meditation is a powerful tool for navigating moments of difficulty and fostering growth.

Whether you're facing emotional triggers, seeking clarity, or celebrating a breakthrough, guided meditations can help you center yourself and connect with your inner wisdom.

In this bonus chapter, you'll find a selection of short, guided meditations designed to support you in specific moments of your healing journey. These practices are simple, accessible, and can be tailored to fit your unique needs.

1. Meditation for Emotional Triggers

Purpose: To ground yourself and regain emotional balance when feeling triggered.

Duration: 5–10 minutes.

Instructions:

- Find a quiet space where you won't be disturbed. Sit comfortably and close your eyes.
- Take a deep breath in through your nose, hold it for a count of four, and exhale slowly through your mouth. Repeat this three times.
- Place your hand over your heart and silently say:

"I am safe. I am here. This moment will pass."

- Visualize yourself standing in a peaceful place, surrounded by light. Imagine the trigger as a wave passing by, receding further with each breath.
- When you feel calmer, take a moment to express gratitude to yourself for pausing and grounding.

2. Meditation for Forgiveness

Purpose: To release resentment and foster compassion, either for yourself or someone else.

Duration: 10–15 minutes.

Instructions:

- Sit in a comfortable position and close your eyes. Take three slow, deep breaths.
- Visualize the person you want to forgive (or yourself) standing in front of you. Imagine a soft, warm light surrounding them.
- Silently say:

"I release the hold this pain has on me. I choose freedom and peace."

- Picture a cord connecting you to them. When you feel ready, imagine gently cutting the cord, watching it dissolve into the light.
- End by repeating:

"I am free. I am whole. I am at peace."

3. Meditation for Self-Love

Purpose: To nurture self-compassion and build confidence.

Duration: 5–10 minutes.

Instructions:

- Find a mirror or sit in a comfortable position where you can focus inward.
- Close your eyes and place your hands over your heart. Take a few deep breaths.
- Silently or aloud, repeat affirmations such as:

"I am enough just as I am."

"I deserve love, kindness, and respect."

"I honor my growth and celebrate my journey."

- Visualize a warm, golden light filling your heart and spreading throughout your body, radiating self-love and acceptance.

4. Meditation for Setting Intentions

Purpose: To align your thoughts and actions with your goals and values.

Duration: 10 minutes.

Instructions:

- Sit in a quiet space and close your eyes. Take a few deep breaths, letting go of tension with each exhale.
- Reflect on what you want to focus on today, this week, or in the coming months.
- Silently say:

"My intention is [state your goal or focus]. I align my actions with my values and purpose."

- Picture yourself moving through your day or week with clarity, confidence, and ease, achieving what you've set out to do.
- End by taking three deep breaths and opening your eyes, ready to take action.

5. Meditation for Gratitude

Purpose: To shift your focus toward positivity and abundance.

Duration: 5 minutes.

Instructions:

- Sit comfortably and take a deep breath in, letting it out slowly.
- Reflect on three things you're grateful for today—big or small. Visualize each one in detail, noticing how they make you feel.
- Silently say:

"I am thankful for [state what you're grateful for]."

- Imagine a sense of warmth and appreciation filling your body, radiating outward.
- End with a deep breath and a smile, carrying that gratitude into the rest of your day.

Final Thoughts

Meditation is a versatile practice that can support you in moments of difficulty, clarity, or celebration. These guided meditations are starting points—feel free to adapt them to your unique needs and experiences. By incorporating them into your routine, you create space for healing, growth, and empowerment in every moment of your journey.

Remember, each time you pause to meditate, you're honoring yourself and your commitment to living as your authentic, empowered self.

Affirmations to Reclaim Your Power

Affirmations are powerful statements that can help shift your mindset, reinforce positive beliefs, and remind you of your inner strength. By repeating affirmations daily, you can challenge limiting thoughts, build confidence, and align yourself with your true potential.

In this chapter, you'll find a curated list of affirmations designed to help you reclaim your power, nurture self-love, and embrace your authentic self. Use them as part of your morning routine, during moments of reflection, or whenever you need a boost of positivity.

Affirmations for Self-Worth

- I am worthy of love, respect, and abundance.
- I am enough just as I am.
- My value is not defined by others' opinions.
- I deserve to take up space and be heard.
- I am proud of who I am becoming.

Affirmations for Resilience and Strength

- I have the strength to overcome any challenge.
- My past does not define me; it empowers me.
- I trust my ability to handle life's obstacles with grace.

- Each step I take brings me closer to my goals.
- I am resilient, resourceful, and capable.

Affirmations for Emotional Healing

- I release the pain of the past and embrace the present.
- It is safe for me to feel and express my emotions.
- I forgive myself for past mistakes and allow myself to grow.
- I let go of resentment and welcome peace into my heart.
- Healing is a journey, and I honor every step I take.

Affirmations for Authenticity

- I am true to myself in all that I do.
- My voice matters, and I use it with confidence.
- I align my actions with my values and purpose.
- I am free to be my authentic self, unapologetically.
- I celebrate my uniqueness and honor my journey.

Affirmations for Setting Boundaries

- I have the right to say no without guilt.
- My time and energy are valuable, and I protect them.
- I create healthy boundaries that support my well-being.
- I surround myself with people who respect and uplift me.
- Saying no is an act of self-love and empowerment.

Affirmations for Abundance and Joy

- I welcome abundance into all areas of my life.
- I deserve to experience joy and happiness every day.
- I attract opportunities that align with my goals and values.
- My life is filled with gratitude, peace, and love.

- I celebrate the beauty and blessings in my life.

Tips for Using Affirmations

Say Them Aloud:

Speaking affirmations out loud reinforces their impact. Say them in front of a mirror to strengthen their connection to your self-image.

Write Them Down:

Keep a journal of affirmations or write them on sticky notes to place around your home or workspace.

Repeat Regularly:

Incorporate affirmations into your morning or evening routine. Repetition helps embed them into your subconscious.

Personalize Them:

Modify affirmations to make them feel authentic to your experiences and goals.

Pair with Visualization:

As you say each affirmation, visualize yourself embodying the belief or achieving the outcome it describes.

Final Thoughts

Affirmations are more than words—they're a declaration of your commitment to growth, healing, and empowerment. By using these affirmations consistently, you remind yourself of your worth, strength, and potential, creating a foundation of positivity and resilience for your journey.

You hold the power to transform your life, and these affirmations are a tool to help you claim that power every day.

Sacred Self-Care Checklist

Self-care is more than a series of tasks—it's a sacred commitment to honoring your mind, body, and spirit. Creating a personal self-care routine ensures that you consistently nurture yourself, recharge your energy, and maintain balance in your daily life. This chapter provides a practical, step-by-step guide to building your own sacred self-care practice, tailored to your unique needs and goals.

Why Self-Care Matters

Self-care is essential for:

- *Emotional Well-Being:* It provides space to process feelings and reduce stress.
- *Physical Health:* Regular care promotes better sleep, energy, and overall vitality.
- *Spiritual Growth:* Self-care rituals can deepen your connection to your inner self and higher purpose.
- *Preventing Burnout:* Taking time for yourself helps you maintain resilience in the face of life's challenges.

Steps to Create Your Personal Self-Care Routine

Assess Your Needs:

Take a moment to reflect on the areas of your life that feel out of balance.

....

....

Ask yourself:

What do I need to feel whole and supported?

....

....

Which activities help me recharge physically, emotionally, and spiritually?

....

....

....

Set Realistic Goals:

Start small by incorporating one or two self-care practices into your routine. Gradually add more as you build consistency.

Prioritize Time for Yourself:

Schedule self-care like any other important appointment. Even 10–15 minutes a day can make a difference.

Honor Your Preferences:

Choose practices that resonate with you. Self-care should feel enjoyable and meaningful, not like a chore.

Sacred Self-Care Checklist

Here's a checklist of ideas to inspire your personal routine. Customize it to fit your lifestyle and needs.

Daily Practices:

☐ Spend 5–10 minutes meditating or practicing deep breathing.

☐ Write one thing you're grateful for in a journal.

☐ Drink enough water to stay hydrated.

☐ Move your body through gentle exercise, stretching, or a walk.

☐ Take a moment to disconnect from technology and enjoy silence.

Weekly Practices:

☐ Set aside time for a longer self-care activity, like a bath or yoga session.

☐ Reflect on your week by journaling about your wins and challenges.

☐ Declutter a small space in your home to create a sense of calm.

☐ Connect with a loved one for a meaningful conversation.

☐ Engage in a creative activity, such as drawing, cooking, or playing music.

Monthly Practices:

☐ Treat yourself to something special, like a favorite meal or a small gift.

☐ Review your goals and adjust them based on your current needs.

☐ Spend time in nature to recharge and reconnect.

☐ Dedicate a day to rest and relaxation without guilt.

☐ Perform a ritual of release, such as burning a list of worries or fears.

Occasional Practices:

☐ Plan a self-care retreat day, where you focus entirely on activities that bring you joy and peace.

☐ Explore a new hobby or interest to spark creativity.

☐ Seek support from a therapist, coach, or mentor when needed.

☐ Organize a small celebration for your accomplishments, no matter how big or small.

☐ Revisit your self-care routine to ensure it still aligns with your needs and goals.

Tips for Maintaining Your Self-Care Routine

Listen to Your Body and Mind:

Pay attention to what you need each day and adjust your routine accordingly.

....

....

Be Flexible:

Life happens, and some days will be busier than others. Focus on what you can do rather than what you can't.

....

....

Avoid Comparison:

Your self-care routine is personal—what works for someone else may not work for you, and that's okay.

Celebrate Consistency:

Acknowledge yourself for showing up, even in small ways. Progress is more important than perfection.

Final Thoughts

Sacred self-care is an ongoing practice of honoring your needs and prioritizing your well-being. By creating a routine that reflects your values and preferences, you nurture yourself on every level—physically, emotionally, and spiritually.

Use this checklist as a starting point, and remember: self-care is not selfish; it's essential. When you care for yourself, you're better equipped to show up fully in all areas of your life. Your well-being is sacred—treat it as such.

Conclusion: Embracing Your Journey

Your journey through this book has been a powerful exploration of your inner world—an act of courage, self-love, and transformation. By confronting your shadow, you've embraced the parts of yourself that may have been hidden, silenced, or overlooked. You've reclaimed your power, healed deep wounds, and begun to write a new story, one rooted in authenticity, resilience, and joy.

This is not the end of your journey; it is a milestone on a lifelong path of growth and self-discovery. You've equipped yourself with tools, rituals, and practices to navigate challenges and celebrate your victories. You've learned that healing is not linear, and progress is not about perfection but about showing up for yourself, day by day, moment by moment.

The Power of Your Shadow Work

Shadow Work has allowed you to see yourself fully—light and shadow, strength and vulnerability. It has shown you that:

- ***Your pain is not your enemy:*** It is a teacher, guiding you toward deeper understanding and growth.
- ***Your emotions are valid:*** Anger, sadness, joy, and love all have a place in your healing journey.
- ***Your story is yours to write:*** No matter what has happened in the past, you have the power to shape your present and future.

This process has connected you to your ancestors, your inner wisdom, and your community. You've tapped into a wellspring of strength that has always been within you, waiting to be acknowledged and celebrated.

Living as Your Authentic Self

To live authentically means to honor your truth, even when it feels uncomfortable or unfamiliar. It means showing up as your whole self, unapologetically, and trusting that you are enough.

Living authentically requires:

- ***Courage:*** To face your fears, set boundaries, and speak your truth.
- ***Self-Compassion:*** To forgive yourself for past mistakes and celebrate your growth.
- ***Intentionality:*** To align your actions with your values and prioritize what truly matters to you.

By embracing your authentic self, you give others permission to do the same. Your authenticity becomes a beacon, inspiring those around you to step into their own truth.

A Legacy of Healing

Your healing journey is not just for you—it is a gift to your family, your community, and future generations. By breaking cycles of pain and rewriting your narrative, you're creating a legacy of empowerment and resilience.

Imagine the ripple effects of your work:

- A child who learns that it's okay to express their emotions because you showed them how.
- A friend who feels inspired to start their own healing journey because you shared your story.
- A future generation that inherits not just pain but the tools to transform it into power.

Your healing is an act of love, and that love will echo far beyond your lifetime.

Staying Committed to Your Journey

Healing is not a one-time event; it is an ongoing practice. As you move forward, remember:

- ***Progress, not perfection:*** Some days will be harder than others, and that's okay. Celebrate every step you take, no matter how small.
- ***Self-care is sacred:*** Make time to nurture your body, mind, and spirit. You deserve rest, joy, and peace.
- ***Stay curious:*** Your shadow will continue to reveal new layers as you grow. Embrace this process as an opportunity for deeper understanding and connection.
- ***Seek support***: Healing is personal, but it doesn't have to be solitary. Lean on trusted friends, family, or professionals when you need guidance or encouragement.

A Call to Action

Take a moment to reflect on how far you've come. You've faced your fears, explored your emotions, and embraced your authentic self. You've begun to transform pain into power, anger into purpose, and silence into strength.

Now, it's time to carry these lessons forward:

- Share your journey with others.
- Honor your needs and boundaries.
- Continue to grow, heal, and celebrate yourself.

Remember, your journey is unique, and there is no "right" way to heal. Trust that you are exactly where you need to be, and know that every step you take is meaningful.

Final Affirmation

Repeat this to yourself as you move forward:

I am whole, worthy, and powerful. I honor my journey and celebrate my growth. My story is mine to write, and I choose to write it with courage, love, and authenticity.

Parting Thoughts

The work you've done is extraordinary. By committing to your healing, you've created space for joy, peace, and abundance in your life. You've proven that you are capable of transformation, and that your power is limitless.

As you close this book, know that this is not an ending—it's a beginning. You have everything you need to live fully, love deeply, and shine brightly. Step into your future with confidence, because the best is yet to come.

You are powerful. You are resilient. You are enough.

Now go forward and live as your most authentic, radiant self. The world needs your light.